Reading Trek!

Noriko Kurihara   Anthony Allan

KINSEIDO

Kinseido Publishing Co., Ltd.
3-21 Kanda Jimbo-cho, Chiyoda-ku,
Tokyo 101-0051, Japan

Copyright © 2019 by Noriko Kurihara
　　　　　　　　 Anthony Allan

*All rights reserved. No part of this publication
may be reproduced, stored in a retrieval system, or
transmitted, in any form or by any means, electronic,
mechanical, photocopying, recording or otherwise,
without the prior permission of the publisher.*

First published 2019 by Kinseido Publishing Co., Ltd.

Cover design　Takayuki Minegishi
Text design　　guild inc.
Illusrations　　Hayato Kamoshita

Acknowledgements to the writers
　　　　Part I　　Keith Kellett, Jiahui Tan, Shaikh Azizur Rahman
　　　　Part II　 Shaikh Azizur Rahman, Ming E. Wong, Keith Kellett, Truthbook.com
　　　　Part III　Jiahui Tan, Ming E. Wong, Keith Kellett, Nyamutatanga Makombe
　　　　Part IV　Keith Kellett, Nyamutatanga Makombe, Jiahui Tan, Leon Schwarzbaum

出典　　Part I　Stories of Miracles
　　　　『English Plus 2011 年春（5 月）号』成美堂出版
　　　　Part II　Touching Stories of Life
　　　　『English Plus 2010 年秋（11 月）号』成美堂出版
　　　　Part III　True Stories of Success
　　　　『English Plus 2012 年冬（2 月）号』成美堂出版
　　　　Part IV　Heroes Among Us
　　　　『English Plus 2013 年春（5 月）号』成美堂出版

音声ファイル無料ダウンロード

http://www.kinsei-do.co.jp/download/4081

この教科書で ◎ DL 00 の表示がある箇所の音声は、上記 URL または QR コードにて無料でダウンロードできます。自習用音声としてご活用ください。

▶ PC からのダウンロードをお勧めします。スマートフォンなどでダウンロードされる場合は、ダウンロード前に「解凍アプリ」をインストールしてください。
▶ URL は、検索ボックスではなくアドレスバー (URL 表示欄) に入力してください。
▶ お使いのネットワーク環境によっては、ダウンロードできない場合があります。

◎ CD 00　左記の表示がある箇所の音声は、教室用 CD（Class Audio CD）に収録されています。

はしがき

Reading Trek! は、世界各地の感動的な物語を厳選し、英語を学ぶ人たちへ向けて、人々の生き方や思いについて読み取り、英文を深く理解するためのエクササイズをつけて編纂したものです。選んだ物語は、アメリカ、イギリス、ドイツ、インド、タイ、ヨルダン、ジンバブエ、中国などを舞台にしており、文化、歴史、宗教、戦争と平和などに関わる様々な人の生き方が描かれています。

本書は15章構成で、各章は Match the Meanings, Discover the Story, Check Your Comprehension, Useful Expressions from the Story, Your Thoughts on the Story の5つのセクションで構成されています。物語の英文は、世界のライターによる原文を単語の難易度と構文の複雑さの観点から解析し、語彙の難易度も調整して再編集したものです。複雑すぎる構文は平易なものへと変更し、書き換えができない語には注をつけました。

本書の活動は、英語で読み進めるということを最重要目標としています。最初のウォームアップとなる語彙問題の Match the Meanings では、本文で使われている重要な語句について、英語での定義を合わせるという形式にしました。Discover the Story で物語を読んだあと、内容理解を問う Check Your Comprehension に進みます。問題は A, B, C の3つのパターンを準備しました。最初の問題 A では、物語の要点となる内容について英語の問いに英語で答える形式で、物語の概要を把握できるようになっています。問題 B は選択問題になっており、正確に詳細を理解できる力を養うためのものです。そして問題 C は真偽を答える問題で、英文全体の内容を深く把握するためのセクションです。次の Useful Expressions from the Story は空所補充問題で、英文で学んだ表現を確認し、しっかりと身につけるためのものです。最後に Your Thoughts on the Story では、英文読解を通じて自分が考えたことや感じたことについて英語で表現するという機会を設けました。考えを整理しやすいように、フォーマットが準備されています。物語について、気に入った点、心を動かされた点とその理由、そしてその物語が自分に与えた影響について書きます。この形式に慣れると、いつでも自分の考えや感想を英語で述べることができるようになるでしょう。

本書は、大学生の皆さんが、心が豊かになるような英語の物語に触れ、共感し、考え、楽しみながら学ぶことを願って作りました。一歩一歩自分の足で世界を旅するように、物語を通して皆さんの世界が広がっていくことを願っております。最後になりましたが、本書の作成にあたり金星堂の皆さんに多大なるご協力とご支援を賜りました。ここに謝意を表します。

栗原典子
Anthony Allan

Reading Trek!

Table of Contents

Part I Stories of Miracles

- Story 1 **Seeing with Sound** ［アメリカ］ ······ 5
  音で見た少年
- Story 2 **Cobra Villages** ［インド］ ······ 10
  コブラと共に生きる村
- Story 3 **Magic or Men?** ［イギリス］ ······ 15
  ストーンヘンジの奇跡
- Story 4 **May's Silent Promise** ［アメリカ］ ······ 20
  最後の時の過ごし方

Part II Touching Stories of Life

Story 5	**The Mystery Word** ［アメリカ］ ········· 25
	祖父母をつないだ謎のことば

Story 6	**Home is Home** ［ヨルダン］ ··········· 30
	ペトラの老女

Story 7	**Mr. Mollah's Birds** ［インド］ ········· 35
	モラーおじさんの鳥

Part III True Stories of Success

Story 8	**Rising from Rock Bottom** ［イギリス］ ········· 40
	世界を変えた想像力

Story 9	**A Man of Many Hats** ［ドイツ］ ········· 45
	現代の万能人

Story 10	**Jiri's Legacy** ［ジンバブエ］ ··········· 50
	ひとりの思いが社会を動かす

Story 11	**From Rags to Riches** ［中国］ ········· 55
	ある富豪の人生

Part IV Heroes Among Us

Story 12	**Priceless Courage** ［アメリカ］ ········· 60
	勇気の炎

Story 13	**Another Battle** ［イギリス］ ··········· 65
	戦いは戦争の後に

Story 14	**Nehanda's Bones** ［ジンバブエ］ ········· 70
	ネハンダの骨

Story 15	**A Trickle Effect** ［アメリカ］ ········· 75
	文化の違いを越えて

Story 1

Seeing with Sound

Match the Meanings

以下の単語の意味を選びましょう。

Match each word (1~10) with the correct definition (a~j).   DL 02   CD1-02

1. remove (v)   [   ]   **a.** to give someone the desire to do something
2. vision (n)   [   ]   well
3. surgery (n)   [   ]   **b.** a machine used for carrying people or goods
4. determined (adj)   [   ]   **c.** to take something away from or out of a place
5. attitude (n)   [   ]   **d.** to make a short, sharp sound
6. click (v)   [   ]   **e.** to move quickly up or back from a surface
7. bounce (v)   [   ]   after hitting it
8. vehicle (n)   [   ]   **f.** a point of view that is influenced by your
9. perspective (n)   [   ]   beliefs or experiences
10. inspire (v)   [   ]   **g.** a particular way of thinking or feeling that is
                                     shown in your behavior
                               h. having a firm decision to do something
                               i. the ability to see with your eyes
                               j. medical treatment of injuries or diseases that
                                     involves cutting open a body

Discover the Story

1 California-native Ben Underwood was just like any other American teenager: he loved to ride his bike, play basketball with his friends, rollerblade and play video games. The only thing he was missing was a pair of eyes.

2 Ben was only two years old when a rare form of cancer was found in both of his eyes. In order to save his life, doctors had no choice but to remove them, which obviously meant losing his sense of vision. When little Ben woke up from the surgery, he was confused, so his mother put his hands on her face and said, "You can't use your eyes anymore, but you have your hands, your nose and your ears." She was determined to never be overprotective of her son, place any limits on him or allow him to feel sorry for himself. She wanted him to live life freely and with a positive attitude.

3 Soon, Ben started to develop a unique skill to get around his home and neighborhood safely. By making sharp clicking noises with his tongue and carefully listening to the sounds that bounced off nearby objects, such as tables and chairs at home, and trees, vehicles and buildings outside, he learned to "see" what was around him. It was a technique called echolocation, and is used by dolphins and bats, but rarely by humans.

4 By the time Ben was in his teens, he had mastered this ability so well that he could correctly tell one shape from another and name the number of small objects placed in front of him without touching them. The skill helped him to enjoy his daily life in safety, since by quickly clicking with his tongue and hearing the echoes, he was able to avoid objects while walking, riding his bike or skating on his rollerblades. Ben had a unique perspective on his situation: "I am not blind. I just can't see," he'd say.

5 Ben's unusual talent and his positive feelings about life acted as

an inspiration to many. The active teenager appeared on a number of TV programs and in various magazines, traveling across the country and abroad, including to his favorite overseas country, Japan. Hoping to go to college there, he even started to teach himself Japanese.

6 However, at the age of 15, Ben's cancer returned. After a brave fight with the disease, on January 19, 2009—a week before his 17th birthday—Ben passed away at home, surrounded by his family. Although he is no longer on this earth, his story continues to inspire and touch the hearts of people around the world.

Notes | **sense of vision**「視覚」　**echolocation**「エコロケーション、反響定位」コウモリやイルカが自らの発した超音波の反射を捉えることで物体の位置を知る方法（能力）

Check Your Comprehension

A 本文の内容について、質問に英語で答えましょう。
Answer each question in English.

1. How was Ben Underwood different from other American teenagers?

2. What happened to Ben when he was two years old?

3. Why did Ben's mother decide to place no limits on him?

4. What unique skill did Ben develop?

5. What did Ben think of his situation?

B 本文の内容について、質問の答えとして最も適切なものを選びましょう。
Choose the best answer for each question.

1. How did the doctors save Ben's life when his cancer was found?
   a. By giving him a lot of encouragement
   b. By removing the cancer through an operation
   c. By giving him a special kind of medicine
   d. By teaching him how to fight against the disease

2. What did Ben's mother think was the most important thing for Ben?
   a. To understand that he was unable to see things
   b. To realize that he was able to see things if he used a special skill
   c. To understand how hard life is without the use of eyes
   d. To realize that he was able to enjoy his life as he liked

3. How could Ben get around inside and outside of his house?
   a. By making clicking sounds and listening to the sounds that bounce off close objects
   b. By listening to the clicking sounds that nearby animals make
   c. By carefully listening to the sounds around him
   d. By making sharp noises and communicating with animals such as bats

4. What ability did Ben have before he became a teenager?
   a. The ability to know what other people want
   b. The ability to identify the shape of objects placed in front of him without touching them
   c. The ability to say the name of objects that other people are talking about
   d. The ability to distinguish the shape of one object from another when he touched them

5. What influence did Ben's life have on people?
   a. Many people felt sorry for him.
   b. Many people were touched by his mother's way of life.
   c. Many people were inspired by his story even after his death.
   d. Many people were surprised by his unusual talent.

C 本文の内容と一致していれば T と、一致していなければ F と答えましょう。
Mark each sentence true (T) or false (F).

1. Ben Underwood was good at playing video games but was unable to ride a bike. [ ]
2. Ben was confused after the surgery because his mother put his hands on his face. [ ]
3. Ben learned to move around his neighborhood safely without doing anything special. [ ]
4. The skill that Ben developed is often used by dolphins and bats but not by humans. [ ]
5. Ben started learning Japanese to study at a Japanese college. [ ]

Useful Expressions from the Story

空所に本文から適切な語を補い、英文を完成させましょう。
Fill in each blank with an appropriate word from the story.

1. He was so determined that we had no _____ but to follow him.
2. He easily gets lost anywhere because he has no _____ of direction.
3. She is a little _____ of her son, so he can't do anything by himself.
4. The heart _____ as a pump.
5. My father had already _____ away when I was born.

Your Thoughts on the Story

本文を読んで感じたことを、英語で書いてみましょう。必要に応じて、以下のフォーマットも活用しましょう。
Write down how you felt about the story after reading it. Use the format below if needed.

What I liked about the story is _____.

I was impressed by _____ because

_____.

After reading this story I thought _____

_____.

Story 2
Cobra Villages

Match the Meanings

以下の単語の意味を選びましょう。

Match each word (1~10) with the correct definition (a~j). DL 04 CD1-09

1. fierce (adj) [ ]
2. threat (n) [ ]
3. inhabit (v) [ ]
4. district (n) [ ]
5. slide (v) [ ]
6. incarnation (n) [ ]
7. apply (v) [ ]
8. wound (n) [ ]
9. identify (v) [ ]
10. swelling (n) [ ]

a. to recognize or distinguish something
b. an injury or damage to part of the body
c. to move smoothly and quietly using the body
d. to live in or occupy an area or place
e. a state of living in a particular form
f. to put or spread something such as liquid or cream onto a surface
g. angry or aggressive and ready to attack
h. a particular area of a country or a town
i. a danger that is likely to cause harm or trouble
j. a place on your body that has become larger than normal as the result of illness or injury

Discover the Story

1 The cobra is known around the world as an extremely fierce and venomous snake. It aggressively attacks anyone it considers its enemy. In South Asia, thousands of people die from snakebites every year, and cobras are involved in more than 30 percent of those life-ending snakebites.

2 Whenever a cobra senses a nearby threat, it spreads its neck to make a hood. Then it targets and shoots its venom at the threat using its fangs. Because of this danger, people tend to stay away from areas where cobras live, and in most places try to kill cobras whenever they find them. The snakes, too, prefer to avoid places inhabited by humans.

3 However, in a group of three villages in the eastern Indian state of West Bengal, cobras are a big part of the villagers' everyday lives—and yet they are anything but deadly. Covering an area of 4-5 square kilometers, the villages in the Bardhaman district are home to at least 6,000 cobras. The villagers and the cobras do not fear each other. In fact, nearly two out of every three of the Bardhaman cobras live inside the rooms or yards of the villagers.

4 Except during winter when the snakes go underground to sleep, at least every second house in the three Bardhaman villages has a cobra lying quietly beneath the bed or in the kitchen. The snake is like a pet cat or dog, largely uninterested in the people around it. At night, some of the Bardhaman cobras even have a habit of sliding up and onto the beds of villagers. Such a situation does not worry the villagers at all. To them, the snakes are not cobras at all, but Jhankeswaree—the living incarnation of a snake goddess.

5 Around 50 people get bitten by the Bardhaman cobras every year, but miraculously, none in the past 20 years has died from a bite or needed medical treatment. When people do get bitten, they are taken to the chief priest of the local Jhankeswaree temple. There, the priest applies some mud from the temple pond to the wound and sings some special songs in praise of the snake goddess. The villagers believe that this process kills the venom immediately.

6 However, following their visit to the Bardhaman villages some years ago, some snake experts from the Zoological Survey of India (ZSI) identified the snakes as the common Indian cobra, scientifically called naja naja. The experts reported that they were indeed deadly cobras—they had all of their fangs, their glands were filled with venom, and their bites could kill one human being within one or two hours.

7 Since the villagers do show some physical reaction after being bitten by the cobras, such as swelling and low fever, the ZSI experts believed that the Bardhaman cobras release only a tiny amount of venom that is not deadly to the human body. The scientists also added that the reason why the Bardhaman cobras do not aggressively attack anyone with larger amounts of venom from their fangs is indeed a mystery.

Notes | **venomous**「毒液を分泌する」　**hood**「(鳥や動物などの) 色のついた頭部」
fangs「牙、毒牙」　**the Zoological Survey of India (ZSI)**「インド動物調査局」
インド政府により1961年に創設された国内の動物の調査と研究を促進するための国内最高の動物研究機関　**glands**「腺、分泌腺」

Check Your Comprehension

A 本文の内容について、質問に英語で答えましょう。
Answer each question in English.

1. What does a cobra do when it finds a nearby threat?

2. What do most people in the world do when they find cobras?

3. How are cobras treated in the houses of the three Bardhaman villages?

4. What kind of treatment do people get when they are bitten by the Bardhaman cobras?

5. What did experts believe is the reason that the villagers were not killed by the Bardhaman cobras?

B 本文の内容について、質問の答えとして最も適切なものを選びましょう。
Choose the best answer for each question.

1. What do people in the world think cobras are like?
   a. They are quiet and smooth.
   b. They are violent and poisonous.
   c. They are a little dangerous.
   d. They are mysterious.

2. How many cobras live with or very close to humans in the three Bardhaman villages?
   a. Not less than six thousand
   b. Nearly six thousand
   c. Almost four thousand
   d. At least two thousand

3. What do people in the three Bardhaman villages consider cobras in their district to be?
   a. Extremely fierce and venomous snakes
   b. Common Indian cobras
   c. The living incarnation of a snake goddess
   d. Their dangerous enemy

4. Who takes care of the Bardhaman villagers that get bitten by cobras?
   a. A doctor who lives in the city
   b. The chief of the village
   c. A housewife who knows a special treatment for snakebites
   d. The chief priest

5. What do the experts think is the reason for Bardhaman cobras not releasing large amounts of venom?
   a. The villagers like the cobras.
   b. The cobras are not afraid of the villagers.
   c. The cobras are truly an incarnation of Jhankeswaree.
   d. They don't know, so it's still a mystery.

C 本文の内容と一致していれば T と、一致していなければ F と答えましょう。
Mark each sentence true (T) or false (F).

1. In South Asia, every year more than half of all snakebite victim deaths are caused by cobras. [ ]
2. Generally, both cobras and humans tend to avoid living close to each other. [ ]
3. People in the three Bardhaman villages do not fear cobras that slide up and onto their beds. [ ]
4. Those who get bitten by the Bardhaman cobras don't die but need medical treatment. [ ]
5. The Bardhaman cobras look the same as common Indian cobras, but have been scientifically identified as different snakes. [ ]

Useful Expressions from the Story

空所に本文から適切な語を補い、英文を完成させましょう。
Fill in each blank with an appropriate word from the story.

1. The cat died _____ the wound.
2. I don't feel like getting involved _____ any New Year's celebrations.
3. Young people _____ to prefer big cities to small towns.
4. He is _____ but a scholar. He knows nothing.
5. They sang the song _____ praise of his courage.

Your Thoughts on the Story

本文を読んで感じたことを、英語で書いてみましょう。必要に応じて、以下のフォーマットも活用しましょう。
Write down how you felt about the story after reading it. Use the format below if needed.

What I liked about the story is _____.

I was impressed by _____ because

_____.

After reading this story I thought _____

_____.

Story 3
Magic or Men?

Match the Meanings

以下の単語の意味を選びましょう。

Match each word (1~10) with the correct definition (a~j).

1. theory (n)   [   ]
2. transport (v)   [   ]
3. alien (n)   [   ]
4. cite (v)   [   ]
5. wizard (n)   [   ]
6. legendary (adj)   [   ]
7. site (n)   [   ]
8. persuade (v)   [   ]
9. feat (n)   [   ]
10. raft (n)   [   ]

a. a creature from another planet or world
b. a man who has magic powers
c. to carry people or goods from one place to another
d. to quote something as a reason or an example
e. an area where something such as a statue or building stands or used to stand
f. an achievement or a result of an action that needs skill, strength or courage
g. described in stories from ancient times
h. to make someone do something by giving good reasons
i. a flat boat made of pieces of wood
j. an idea that someone believes is true but has not yet been proved

Discover the Story

1 Many people travel from all over the world to see the ancient stone circle at Stonehenge in England. It is said that all the known facts about the circle could be typed on a single sheet of paper, and everything else is theory and guesswork. Nobody, for instance, knows the exact purpose of the stones, and we can only guess how they came to be there.

2 The circle was made using two types of stone. One type is called "sarsen," and the nearest place where it can be found is in Lockeridge Dene, 50 kilometers away. The other type, called "bluestone," comes from the Preseli Hills in Wales, which is even farther away, on the other side of the Bristol Channel.

3 So, how was the stone transported to its present location? Experiments have been conducted over the years to see if early man could indeed have carried out such a task. Several methods have been tried, and all have had some measure of success. Bluestone stones have actually been found at the bottom of the Bristol Channel, suggesting that they may well have been transported across the water in ancient boats.

4 However, to take on the task of building the circle, a structured organization and an influential leadership was required. For years, it was thought that ancient Britons did not have either of these, so scientists and researchers sometimes imagined that a different method was involved. Even today, some people say that it was beyond the capability of early man to build such a structure and suggest that Earth was visited by aliens who had used their superior technology to lend a hand.

5 An earlier theory was that magical powers were used to construct Stonehenge. Some cited Merlin, the wizard at the legendary English court of King Arthur. It is a very thin link, but some people even claimed that the name of the nearby town, Amesbury, came from Merlin's other names: Emrys or Ambrose.

6 It is highly probable, though, that the stones

were brought to the site by men alone. Someone must have persuaded hundreds or thousands of them that it was necessary to take the stones there. Even so, this still leaves the question of how they achieved such a difficult yet amazing feat. It is likely that the heavy objects, weighing up to 50 tons each, were transported by sledges, rollers, simple rafts and pure muscle power.

 Still, to do such a job—to seek out the source of usable stones and persuade all those people to carry them all that distance for the sake of an idea which we can only guess at—is nothing short of a miracle!

Notes | **sarsen**「サルセン石、大砂岩」第三紀初期のケイ質砂岩の一種；特にイングランドのウィルトシャーの砂丘に点在する **Lockeridge Dene**「ローカリッジ集落」イングランド南西部のウィルトシャー州にある **bluestone**「ブルーストーン」粘土質砂岩；建築・敷石に用いられる **the Preseli Hills**「プレセリ連丘」ウェールズ南西部のペンブルックシャー州にある **the Bristol Channel**「ブリストル海峡」グレイト・ブリテン島にある入江（南ウェールズと南西イングランドのデボンとサマーセットを隔てている）

Check Your Comprehension

A 本文の内容について、質問に英語で答えましょう。
Answer each question in English.

1. Why do people from various countries travel to Stonehenge in England?

2. What is the distance between Stonehenge and the nearest place the stones come from?

3. Why were experiments conducted on how the stones were transported?

4. Why was it thought to have been impossible for men to construct the stone circle at Stonehenge?

5. Why does the writer say in the 6th paragraph, "It is highly probable, though, that the stones were brought to the site by men alone"?

B 本文の内容について、質問の答えとして最も適切なものを選びましょう。
Choose the best answer for each question.

1. What does the following statement in the 1st paragraph mean: "All the known facts about the circle could be typed on a single sheet of paper"?
   a. Everybody knows the facts about the circle.
   b. There are many known facts about the circle.
   c. There are not many people who write facts about Stonehenge.
   d. The number of known facts about the circle is very limited.

2. What does "a different method" in the 4th paragraph refer to?
   a. A method that ancient Greeks used
   b. Advanced technology that was developed on another planet
   c. Advanced technology that modern Britons had
   d. A method that Chinese people developed in ancient times

3. What does "a very thin link" in the 5th paragraph mean?
   a. A very weak connection
   b. A wild imagination
   c. A very unusual relationship
   d. Very poor communication

4. Why did some people believe that the stones were carried by magical powers?
   a. Because they thought it impossible for aliens to carry the heavy stones.
   b. Because they saw Merlin carrying the stones.
   c. Because it was believed the nearby town was named after the famous wizard.
   d. Because the story about King Arthur mentions the stones.

5. Which method was most likely used to transport the stones?
   a. Magical and human powers
   b. Human physical power
   c. Several different vehicles
   d. Advanced technology from creatures from outer space

C 本文の内容と一致していればTと、一致していなければFと答えましょう。
Mark each sentence true (T) or false (F).

1. No one knows why the stones are in Stonehenge. [ ]
2. The stones seem to have been brought from distant places. [ ]
3. The method used to transport the stones to their present site is a total mystery. [ ]
4. Most people today believe that magical powers were used to construct Stonehenge. [ ]
5. Regardless of the theories, the construction of the stones at Stonehenge is a miracle. [ ]

Useful Expressions from the Story

空所に本文から適切な語を補い、英文を完成させましょう。
Fill in each blank with an appropriate word from the story.

1. By the late 70s he had achieved a_____ of fame. [= a degree of]
2. They _____ well have known the fact. [= It is very likely that they knew]
3. I can't _____ on any extra work. [= accept]
4. The neighbors are always willing to lend a _____. [= help]
5. His behavior was nothing _____ of rude. [= nothing but]

Your Thoughts on the Story

本文を読んで感じたことを、英語で書いてみましょう。必要に応じて、以下のフォーマットも活用しましょう。
Write down how you felt about the story after reading it. Use the format below if needed.

What I liked about the story is _____.

I was impressed by _____ because _____.

After reading this story I thought _____.

Story 4
May's Silent Promise

Match the Meanings

以下の単語の意味を選びましょう。

Match each word (1~10) with the correct definition (a~j). DL 08   CD1-25

1. shaman (n)   [   ]
2. incense-filled (adj)   [   ]
3. hut (n)   [   ]
4. swallow (v)   [   ]
5. meteor (n)   [   ]
6. pop into (v)   [   ]
7. stare (v)   [   ]
8. streak (n)   [   ]
9. remote (adj)   [   ]
10. checkup (n)   [   ]

a. a small wooden house with only one or two rooms
b. a medical examination to check your health
c. a person who is believed to have powers to heal sick people or to be able to contact spirits
d. to make food or drink go into your stomach
e. full of the smoke of a burned tree gum or of spice, etc.
f. to enter a place suddenly for a short time
g. far away from places where people live
h. to look at something or someone for a long time
i. burning pieces of rock that come to earth from space
j. a long thin stripe or mark that is a different color from its background

Discover the Story

1 "You'll live to see a long life ahead of you," the Thai village shaman said as he handed the woman a cup of green liquid. Every night after May had helped the women to clear away the food, the shaman would call her to his incense-filled hut. There he'd spend half an hour saying a series of prayers and finally ending them by handing her some herbal liquids that he insisted would help her.

2 This was going to be the last cup of medicine she'd take before leaving the village the following day. As May swallowed the bitter mixture, she felt a silent tear roll down each of her cheeks. Before she could say a thing, she heard a noise outside. "Come and see the meteor shower!" a neighbor said, popping her head into the hut before dashing off to join the others.

3 "Shooting stars! Shooting stars!" a child shouted excitedly as May stared up into the night sky. Many small streaks of light appeared and disappeared as the meteors flashed across the dark sky. Standing in the middle of an open field and surrounded by the excited villagers all looking at the display from heaven, May found a deep warmth filling her soul. At that moment, a strong hand reached over and gently held hers. She looked up at her husband Paul, and felt a smile escape her lips.

4 This was the last day of her five-month stay in the village, but May felt completely at ease. If she died today, she wouldn't care, for she had at least spent the last days of her life with loved ones—and had made a difference to the villagers in this remote Thai village.

5 Things hadn't been this way five months ago. When May found out about her terminal-stage cancer, she lost all interest in life. That was until Paul pulled her out from her self-pity. "Come on, feeling sad is not going to make things better. Let's use this time to make a difference in someone's life," he told her. True to his words, he took one year off work to join her on what she imagined would be her last mission while alive: a volunteer trip to a remote village in

Story 4 | May's Silent Promise

Chiang Mai, Thailand.

6 The day after the magical meteor display, May said a tearful goodbye to the people she had come to think of as family. "If I'm still alive next year, I'll come back to see and help you all," she silently promised herself.

7 As she turned to take a last look at the village, a wrinkled hand reached out through a window and patted her on the arm. It was the shaman. "Yesterday's meteor shower—it was a good sign," he said as he gave her a wave and a nod.

8 When May returned to her home and went to the hospital for her checkup, the doctors were astonished because her cancer had completely disappeared! Since then, 20 years have passed, and May has never missed a year where she has gone back to see the people who she believes drove away her cancer.

Note | **Chiang Mai**「チェンマイ」タイ北部で最大の都市

Check Your Comprehension

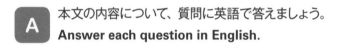

本文の内容について、質問に英語で答えましょう。
Answer each question in English.

1. Who received a cup of green liquid from the Thai village shaman?

2. Why did the shaman call May and spend half an hour saying a series of prayers?

3. Why did May come to the remote Thai village?

4. How many times has May visited the village since her cancer disappeared?

5. What does May believe caused her cancer to disappear?

B 本文の内容について、質問の答えとして最も適切なものを選びましょう。
Choose the best answer for each question.

1. What were the herbal liquids that the shaman handed May?
   a. A special tea for guests
   b. A medicine
   c. A drink for relaxation
   d. A regular tea for workers

2. How did May feel when she was looking up at the shooting stars with the villagers?
   a. She was satisfied with the days she had spent with them.
   b. She felt a pain in her eyes.
   c. She was sad because she would soon leave the village.
   d. She found herself lonely and unhappy.

3. Why did May feel completely at ease on her last day in the village?
   a. She knew she would die very soon anyway.
   b. She knew she would live long and come back to the village again.
   c. She knew she had spent a meaningful time there.
   d. She knew the people she had met would never forget her.

4. How had May been spending her days in the months before she came to the Thai village?
   a. She had been enjoying her life, only thinking of herself.
   b. She had been feeling sorry for herself because of her disease.
   c. She had been in the hospital because she had a serious disease.
   d. She had been working hard despite her disease.

5. What did May find after going back home from the Thai village?
   a. Her disease had not gotten worse.
   b. She had completely recovered from the disease.
   c. It was possible for her to get an operation to remove her cancer.
   d. It was impossible for her to go back to the village again.

C 本文の内容と一致していればTと、一致していなければFと答えましょう。
Mark each sentence true (T) or false (F).

1. Paul left May in Chiang Mai alone. [ ]
2. May didn't stay in Chiang Mai to enjoy sightseeing. [ ]
3. May never thought she would return to the village again. [ ]
4. May believed watching the meteor shower helped her get better. [ ]
5. If Paul hadn't suggested that she go to the Thai village, May would probably have died of cancer soon. [ ]

Useful Expressions from the Story

空所に本文から適切な語を補い、英文を完成させましょう。
Fill in each blank with an appropriate word from the story.

1. Tom _____ away the trash. [= removed]
2. I am quite at_____ among strangers. [= relaxed]
3. The leader's decision _____ a difference in their lives. [= had a significant effect on]
4. _____ to his words, he came to the meeting. [= Keeping his promise]
5. He _____ me on the back. [= touched me in a friendly way]

Your Thoughts on the Story

本文を読んで感じたことを、英語で書いてみましょう。必要に応じて、以下のフォーマットも活用しましょう。
Write down how you felt about the story after reading it. Use the format below if needed.

What I liked about the story is _____.

I was impressed by _____ because

_____.

After reading this story I thought _____

_____

_____.

Story 5

The Mystery Word

Match the Meanings

以下の単語の意味を選びましょう。

Match each word (1~10) with the correct definition (a~j). DL 10 CD1-34

1. feed (v) [ ]
2. unroll (v) [ ]
3. stuff (v) [ ]
4. trace (v) [ ]
5. comfort (v) [ ]
6. funeral (n) [ ]
7. thin (v) [ ]
8. shaky (adj) [ ]
9. grief (n) [ ]
10. witness (v) [ ]

a. to open something that was rolled up
b. a ceremony that is held for burying or burning a dead person
c. physically weak or unstable, because you are nervous, old, or ill
d. to see something happen
e. to become less crowded
f. to give food to eat to a person, group, or animal
g. feeling of extreme sadness, especially caused by someone's death
h. to put something into a small space
i. to draw or mark a line or pattern on a surface
j. to make someone who is worried or unhappy feel better or less worried

Discover the Story

1 My grandparents were married for over half a century, and played their own special game from the time they met each other. The goal of their game was to write a special kind of word, "shmily," in a surprise place for the other to find. They took turns leaving "shmily" around the house, and as soon as one of them
5 discovered the word, it was the other's turn to leave it somewhere else.

2 They wrote "shmily" with their fingers through the sugar and flour in containers and waited for whoever was preparing the next meal. They wrote it with water drops on the windows of the dining room where Grandma always fed us warm homemade pudding. "Shmily" was also written in the steam left on the
10 mirror after a hot shower, where it would re-appear bath after bath. At one point, Grandma even unrolled an entire roll of toilet paper to leave "shmily" on the very last sheet.

3 There was no end to the places "shmily" would pop up. Little notes with "shmily" written hurriedly were found on dashboards and car seats, or taped to steering
15 wheels. The notes were stuffed inside shoes and left under pillows. "Shmily" was also written in the dust on shelves and traced in the morning ashes of the fireplace. This mysterious word was as much a part of my grandparents' house as the furniture.

4 Grandma and Grandpa held hands every chance they could. They finished
20 each other's sentences and shared the crossword puzzle in the daily newspaper. My grandmother often whispered to me about how cute, kind and handsome Grandpa was, even in old age, and proudly claimed that she really knew "how to pick 'em."

5 Before every meal they bowed their heads and gave thanks, since they were
25 so happy for their blessings: a wonderful family and each other.

6 But there was a dark cloud in my grandparents' life: my grandmother had breast cancer. The disease had first
30 appeared ten years earlier. As always, Grandpa was with her every step of the way.

He comforted her in their yellow bedroom, painted that way so she could always be surrounded by sunshine, even when she was too sick to go outside.

7 Now the cancer was again attacking her body. With the help of a walking stick and my grandfather's steady hand, my grandmother went to church every morning. But she grew weaker and weaker until she could no longer leave the house. For a while, Grandpa would go to church alone, praying to God to watch over his wife. Then one day, what we all feared finally happened. Grandma was gone. "Shmily" was written in yellow on the pink ribbons of my grandmother's funeral bouquet.

8 As the crowd thinned and the people turned to leave, family members came forward and gathered around Grandma one last time. Grandpa stepped up to my grandmother's casket and, taking a shaky breath, he began to sing to her. Through his tears and grief, the song came—a deep and rough-sounding lullaby. Shaking with my own sadness, I will never forget that moment. I knew that, although I couldn't begin to understand the depth of their love, I had been lucky to witness its pure beauty. Their special word stood for "See how much I love you."

Notes | **dashboard**「(自動車の) ダッシュボード、計器盤」　　**casket**「棺」
| **lullaby**「子守唄」

Check Your Comprehension

A 本文の内容について、質問に英語で答えましょう。
Answer each question in English.

1. What was the special game for the writer's grandparents?

_____

2. When did they begin to play the game?

_____

3. What was the dark cloud in the grandparents' life?

_____

4. What did the grandfather do at the end of the funeral?

_____

5. What did "shmily" mean?

_____

B 本文の内容について、質問の答えとして最も適切なものを選びましょう。
Choose the best answer for each question.

1. What was "shmily"?
   a. It was a kind of food.
   b. It was a piece of furniture.
   c. It was a book.
   d. It was a special kind of word.

2. What did the writer's grandparents do when they found "shmily"?
   a. They wrote the word again somewhere else.
   b. They erased the word immediately.
   c. They told others that they had found the word.
   d. They waited one week before they played the game again.

3. Which one of the following did the writer's grandparents actually do when they played the special game?
   a. They fed the writer homemade pudding.
   b. They wrote the word in the dust on shelves.
   c. They turned on the shower in the bathroom.
   d. They moved some furniture around.

4. Why did the writer's grandmother unroll an entire roll of toilet paper?
   a. Because she wanted to use up the toilet paper at that time.
   b. Because she suddenly became sick after a hot shower.
   c. Because she wanted to write "shmily" on the last piece of paper.
   d. Because she wanted to write "shmily" all over the toilet roll.

5. Why did the writer's grandfather paint his and his wife's bedroom yellow?
   a. Because he liked the color and it made him happy.
   b. Because his wife liked the color and it helped her to sleep.
   c. Because the doctor said the color might cure his wife's disease.
   d. Because he thought it might make his wife feel surrounded by sunshine.

C 本文の内容と一致していればTと、一致していなければFと答えましょう。
Mark each sentence true (T) or false (F).

1. The writer's grandparents lived together for more than fifty years. [ ]
2. The writer's grandmother didn't hold hands with her husband so often. [ ]
3. The writer's grandmother had stomach cancer. [ ]
4. The writer's grandmother went to church until her last day. [ ]
5. The writer thought he was lucky to witness how beautiful the grandparents' love was. [ ]

Useful Expressions from the Story

空所に本文から適切な語を補い、英文を完成させましょう。
Fill in each blank with an appropriate word from the story.

1. John practiced speaking English every _____ he could get.
2. UN _____ for United Nations.
3. He said he'd cooperate, and actually helped us every _____ of the way.
4. A visit to the moon is no _____ impossible.
5. They _____ turns singing their favorite songs at the party last night.

Your Thoughts on the Story

本文を読んで感じたことを、英語で書いてみましょう。必要に応じて、以下のフォーマットも活用しましょう。
Write down how you felt about the story after reading it. Use the format below if needed.

What I liked about the story is _____.

I was impressed by _____ because

_____.

After reading this story I thought _____

_____

_____.

Story 6

Home is Home

Match the Meanings

以下の単語の意味を選びましょう。

Match each word or phrase (1~10) with the correct definition (a~j).

DL 12　CD1-43

1. attraction (n)　　　[　]
2. cave (n)　　　　　[　]
3. house (v)　　　　　[　]
4. permanently (adv)　[　]
5. official (n)　　　　[　]
6. attention (n)　　　[　]
7. reason with (v)　　[　]
8. atmosphere (n)　　[　]
9. disobey (v)　　　　[　]
10. determination (n)　[　]

a. a strong will to do something
b. a large natural hole in the side of a hill or under the ground
c. for always; until the end of time; forever
d. great interest shown in someone or something
e. to talk to someone to persuade them to be more sensible
f. a person who is in a position of authority in an organization
g. the general feeling of a place or environment
h. to provide space for or contain something
i. to refuse to do what someone tells you to do
j. something that people can go to for interest or fun

Discover the Story

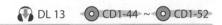

1 The history books tell us that in 1812 Johann Ludwig Burckhardt discovered Petra, the rock city that is presently one of Jordan's major tourist attractions. However, "discovered" may not be the right word, for the local Bedouin people had always been living in the caves there, right up until fairly recently.

2 Some of the caves still house shops and restaurants, although almost nobody lives permanently in Petra now. However, living in a cave is not as bad as it sounds. There are similar places in Tunisia, for example, and they are extremely comfortable.

3 When the Bedouin people of Jordan were sent away to live elsewhere, one elderly lady refused to move. "I was born in this house. I have always lived in this house. And, I shall die in this house," she said with watery eyes.

4 Official after official came to see her but received the same tearful response. She was not going to leave the comfortable, welcoming and familiar home she had always known and loved, even for a modern house in the nearby village of Wadi Musa.

5 Eventually, the matter came to the attention of Jordan's king, King Hussein. He wanted to speak to the lady himself and try to reason with her, but was unable to do so due to his busy schedule. So, he sent his brother, Prince Hassan instead.

6 Following the Bedouin custom, the local people politely welcomed the Prince and served him tea and sweets. The elderly lady tearfully repeated her story to the Prince, and the comfort and welcoming atmosphere of the little cave house were not lost upon him. However, even though he had come to try and persuade the lady, she still would not leave her home.

7 After a while she said she had a gift for the Prince, and left the living room. Soon, she returned with a silver tray covered with a cloth. Under the cloth was a knife, and when the Prince's bodyguards saw it, they quickly reached for their weapons.

8 The elderly lady explained she meant the Prince no harm, but intended the knife as a gift. She said to the Prince, "I've made up my mind that I'm going to die in this house, but I cannot disobey a prince. So please take the knife and kill me now."

9 Prince Hassan was close to tears himself at her honest words. He said she could stay where she was for the moment, and he would speak with the King. Upon hearing the story from the Prince, King Hussein was also deeply moved by the lady's determination and courage, and he immediately ordered that she was to remain in her home until the day she died.

Notes | **Petra**「ペトラ」ヨルダン南部の古代都市（ヘレニズム・ローマ時代のアラブ人の王国の中心）
Bedouin「ベドウィン」アラビア、シリア、北アフリカの砂漠の遊牧のアラブ人

Check Your Comprehension

 本文の内容について、質問に英語で答えましょう。
Answer each question in English.

1. What is Petra today?

2. Why is almost nobody living permanently in Petra today?

3. Why did the elderly lady refuse to move from her home?

4. Why did King Hussein want to speak to the lady himself and try to reason with her?

5. Why did the Prince's bodyguards reach for their weapons when they saw the knife?

B 本文の内容について、質問の答えとして最も適切なものを選びましょう。
Choose the best answer for each question.

1. Where had the local Bedouin people been living until recently?
   a. In Wadi Musa village near Petra
   b. In the caves of the rock city
   c. In the shops and restaurants of Petra
   d. In the caves of Tunisia

2. What did the officials offer the elderly lady if she left the cave?
   a. An apartment near the shops and restaurants in Petra
   b. A comfortable cave in Tunisia
   c. A modern house in Wadi Musa
   d. A house similar to her comfortable, welcoming and familiar home

3. Why did the King send Prince Hassan instead of him?
   a. The King was too busy to speak to the elderly lady.
   b. The King was too afraid to speak to the elderly lady.
   c. The King didn't want to speak to the elderly lady.
   d. The Prince asked the King to send him to talk to the elderly lady.

4. How did the elderly lady respond to the Prince's visit?
   a. She was so happy to see the Prince that she started to cry.
   b. She felt sorry that she had to leave her home eventually.
   c. She was very polite and agreed with what the Prince said.
   d. She cried and refused to leave the cave.

5. Why did the elderly lady bring the knife to the Prince?
   a. She wanted to give the knife to the King as a gift.
   b. She wanted to kill the Prince and his guards.
   c. She wanted to show her determination to die in the cave.
   d. She wanted to tell the Prince that she would leave the cave.

C 本文の内容と一致していればTと、一致していなければFと答えましょう。
Mark each sentence true (T) or false (F).

1. Living in a cave is more comfortable than people might think. [ ]
2. The Bedouin people of Jordan moved to other places because they wanted to. [ ]
3. When the Prince came, the atmosphere of the cave house became less comfortable. [ ]
4. The Prince was moved when he heard the elderly lady speak so honestly. [ ]
5. The King was touched by the elderly lady's courage and allowed her to continue living in the cave. [ ]

Useful Expressions from the Story

空所に本文から適切な語を補い、英文を完成させましょう。
Fill in each blank with an appropriate word from the story.

1. Tom sent the bad guys _____ from the town.
2. Jane arrived late _____ to heavy traffic.
3. My father was too busy to attend the event, so he sent his secretary _____.
4. The girls were close to _____ when they read the sad story.
5. _____ seeing the police, the boys stopped fighting.

Your Thoughts on the Story

本文を読んで感じたことを、英語で書いてみましょう。必要に応じて、以下のフォーマットも活用しましょう。
Write down how you felt about the story after reading it. Use the format below if needed.

What I liked about the story is _____.

I was impressed by _____ because

_____.

After reading this story I thought _____

_____.

Story 7
Mr. Mollah's Birds

Match the Meanings

以下の単語の意味を選びましょう。

Match each word (1~10) with the correct definition (a~j). DL 14　CD1-53

1. tailor (n)　　　[　]
2. cage (n)　　　[　]
3. earnings (n)　 [　]
4. ritual (n)　　 [　]
5. thrive (v)　　 [　]
6. count (v)　　　[　]
7. grain (n)　　　[　]
8. cemetery (n)　 [　]
9. devastated (adj) [　]
10. relieve (v)　 [　]

a. a place that is used for burying dead people
b. the seeds of crops such as wheat, rice, corn, etc. that are harvested and used for food
c. feeling very upset and shocked
d. a person whose job is to make clothes
e. to be important or valuable
f. a structure made of bars or wires in which animals or birds are kept
g. the money you receive for the work you do
h. to remove or reduce an unpleasant feeling or situation
i. something that you do regularly and always in the same way
j. to become successful, strong, healthy, etc.

Discover the Story

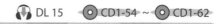

1 Noor Nobi Mollah, a 55-year-old tailor in India, thinks people who keep birds in cages yet regard themselves as bird-lovers are wrong, and every week he puts some of his limited earnings behind his belief.

2 Mr. Mollah makes baby clothes and works up to 15 hours a day in his workshop inside a Kolkata slum. But each Wednesday, on his weekly day off, the tailor performs his most "precious duty"—freeing caged birds.

3 Every Tuesday evening, as soon as his week's production has been bought by wholesalers, Mr. Mollah gives three quarters of his earnings to his wife for the family's daily expenses. He keeps the rest for his Wednesday ritual, which he has been performing for the past 20 years without fail.

4 In the early 1990s, the selling of birds was banned in India. Even so, many bird markets still thrive because police and wildlife officials are bribed. Every week in Kolkata, bird sellers supply up to 6,000 birds that have been caught in nearby villages. And every Wednesday morning, Mr. Mollah is at his local market to buy birds—as many as he can afford. Why does he do this?

5 Whereas the typical "bird-lover" prefers to buy the healthier and more beautiful birds, Mr. Mollah looks for those that have remained unsold for days. "If I go for beautiful birds, I can get less of them in number. Therefore, I look for less colorful and sick or weaker birds. To me, it's lives and not beauty that counts," he says.

6 Every week Mr. Mollah manages to buy 15 or 20 birds with his small amount of money. He then takes the caged birds home to feed them grain and, if they are sick or injured, gives them first aid. Then, in the afternoon, at a nearby cemetery, he takes the birds from their cages one by one and sets them free.

7 Over the past two decades more than 17,000 starlings, sparrows, mynahs and many other birds have had their freedom returned by Mr. Mollah—the kind "Birdman of Kolkata,"

who has never been to school in his life.

8 His unusual ritual comes from a personal tragedy 21 years earlier when an accident took the lives of two of his children and a nephew, leaving him devastated. "To them, death came so easily," he says. "No magical power could return the lost children to life, and in a strange way I strongly realized that life is the most precious thing on the earth. I kept on thinking how I could do something to save a living creature, to relieve it of its pain. Then I thought of releasing birds."

9 Mr. Mollah sits by the grave of the three boys as he frees the birds while saying prayers. "Allah, I can do so little with my limited ability. If you think that I am doing a good job releasing these birds from cages, please keep everyone, including my children, in peace in your heaven—I always say something along these lines when I release the birds," says Mr. Mollah. "I shall keep setting birds free until the last Wednesday of my life."

Notes | **slum**「貧民街」　**wholesaler**「卸売業者、問屋」　**bribe**「賄賂を使う、買収する」
starling「ムクドリ」　**sparrow**「スズメ」　**mynah**「マイナ」ムクドリ科の鳥の一部の総称（ハッカチョウ、キュウカンチョウなど）　**Allah**「アラー、神様」イスラム教の唯一神

Check Your Comprehension

A 本文の内容について、質問に英語で答えましょう。
Answer each question in English.

1. What is Noor Nobi Mollah's belief about bird-lovers?

2. What is Mr. Mollah's most precious duty?

3. How many birds are sold in Kolkata every week?

4. What does Mr. Mollah do to the birds before releasing them?

5. How many birds has Mr. Mollah freed since he started the ritual?

B 本文の内容について、質問の答えとして最も適切なものを選びましょう。
Choose the best answer for each question.

1. What does Mr. Mollah spend one quarter of his earnings on?
    a. Making baby clothes
    b. Buying as many birds as he can
    c. Buying cages to keep his birds
    d. Feeding the birds that he keeps in his home

2. Why are bird markets successful in Kolkata despite the fact that selling birds is banned in India?
    a. There are too many birds in India.
    b. People in India love eating birds.
    c. The police and officials are bribed.
    d. People in India don't like obeying the law.

3. What does Mr. Mollah think is the most important thing when he buys birds?
    a. How many birds he can buy
    b. How beautiful the birds are
    c. How large the birds are
    d. How many colors the birds have

4. Why did Mr. Mollah start his Wednesday morning ritual?
    a. Wildlife officials told him that the selling of birds was banned in India.
    b. He realized that his children and nephew would be pleased with his unusual ritual.
    c. He learned that a lot of birds were caught in nearby villages.
    d. When the boys died, he realized that life is the most precious thing on the earth.

5. What does Mr. Mollah pray for when he frees birds?
    a. Happiness for everyone in the world
    b. Peace for everyone in heaven
    c. Safety for all birds on the earth
    d. Peace for all birds in heaven

C 本文の内容と一致していれば T と、一致していなければ F と答えましょう。
Mark each sentence true (T) or false (F).

1. Mr. Mollah only went to elementary school. [ ]
2. Mr. Mollah has freed thousands of birds over the past two decades. [ ]
3. Mr. Mollah's children and nephew were killed in an accident. [ ]
4. Mr. Mollah buys weaker birds because he doesn't like strong birds. [ ]
5. Mr. Mollah believes magical power will return the lost children if he does something special. [ ]

Useful Expressions from the Story

空所に本文から適切な語を補い、英文を完成させましょう。
Fill in each blank with an appropriate word from the story.

1. He is not wealthy. I don't think he can _____ to buy such an expensive car.
2. Tim is a good son. He visits his mother every day without _____.
3. Any road accident that causes a death or serious injury is a _____.
4. Please _____ seated until your name is called.
5. The prisoners were all _____ free when the fire broke out.

Your Thoughts on the Story

本文を読んで感じたことを、英語で書いてみましょう。必要に応じて、以下のフォーマットも活用しましょう。
Write down how you felt about the story after reading it. Use the format below if needed.

What I liked about the story is _____.

I was impressed by _____ because

_____.

After reading this story I thought _____

_____

_____.

Story 8

Rising from Rock Bottom

Match the Meanings

以下の単語の意味を選びましょう。

Match each word (1~10) with the correct definition (a~j). DL 16　CD1-63

1. serve (v)　　　　[　]
2. interrupt (v)　　[　]
3. welfare (n)　　　[　]
4. manuscript (n)　[　]
5. submit (v)　　　[　]
6. editor (n)　　　　[　]
7. grant (n)　　　　[　]
8. positive (adj)　　[　]
9. adore (v)　　　　[　]
10. foundation (n)　[　]

a. to be useful or helpful in achieving an aim
b. an idea or principle, etc. that something develops from or is based on
c. to stop something for a period of time
d. to feel great love for someone
e. feeling hopeful and confident, and sure that something good will happen
f. money given one time by an organization for a particular purpose
g. a piece of writing before it is printed
h. to give a plan or proposal to someone for judgment
i. a person who decides the content of newspapers, etc.
j. practical or financial help given regularly to poor people by the goverment

40

Discover the Story

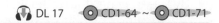

1 Joanne Rowling was born on July 31, 1965 in Yate, Gloucestershire, England. Growing up on a diet of fantasy stories, she had a wonderful imagination which she utilized to come up with bedtime stories to tell her baby sister, Dianne.

2 Her strong imagination continued to serve her well, even as an adult. In 1990, while on a train trip from Manchester to London, she struck upon the idea for a story about a boy attending a school of wizardry. When she arrived at her apartment, she got down to writing it immediately.

3 Her story, however, was interrupted when her mother passed away later that year after a ten-year fight with a terrible disease. Rowling then moved to Porto, Portugal, to teach English as a foreign language. While there, she met and married Portuguese television journalist Jorge Arantes, and their daughter Jessica was born in July 1993.

4 Unfortunately, Rowling's married life was short-lived. In November that year, she separated from her husband and moved back to the UK to be near her sister in Edinburgh, Scotland. However, she fell into clinical depression during this period and even considered ending her life. She had constant feelings of worthlessness and hopelessness since her marriage had failed and she had no job to support her young daughter.

5 Living off welfare payments in unpleasant and "depressing" government housing, Rowling worked passionately on her book as a means of escaping from her awful reality. She would push Jessica around in a stroller until the baby fell asleep and then settle down in cafes to work on her story about the young boy studying magic at school. Working on an old manual typewriter, Rowling managed to come up with a manuscript in 1995 and submitted her work to a total of 12 publishing companies— only to be rejected by all of them.

6 Finally, in 1996 she got a "yes" from the publisher Bloomsbury, although the editor told her she should get a day job, as children's writers rarely make much. Thankfully, an £8,000 grant from the Scottish Arts Council allowed her to continue writing, and *Harry Potter and the Philosopher's Stone* was published on June 30, 1997. This first work became an instant success. At a book fair later that year, Scholastic Books bought the American rights for $105,000, which was a record sum at the time for a children's writer.

7 By the time her fourth book, *Harry Potter and the Goblet of Fire*, came out, Rowling had become the highest-earning woman in Britain, with sales of more than $29.3 million from her books. The popularity of her works has continued to grow since then. Today, the Harry Potter series has sold more than 450 million books worldwide in 67 different languages and has been made into a series of blockbuster films about the boy wizard.

8 For Rowling, her darkest hour had a positive ending. Looking back on her experiences, she said, "Had I really succeeded at anything else, I might never have found the determination to succeed in the one area where I truly belonged. I was set free, because my greatest fear had been realized, and I was still alive, and I still had a daughter whom I adored, and I had an old typewriter and a big idea. And so rock bottom became a solid foundation on which I rebuilt my life."

Notes | **wizardry**「魔法、魔術」　**Portugal**「ポルトガル」　**Portuguese**「ポルトガル人（の）」　**clinical depression**「臨床的抑うつ」　**stroller**「ベビーカー」　**The Scottish Arts Council**「スコットランド芸術審議会」　*Harry Potter and the Philosopher's Stone*「『ハリー・ポッターと賢者の石』」　*Harry Potter and the Goblet of Fire*「『ハリー・ポッターと炎のゴブレット』」　**blockbuster**「大ヒット作（映画、本など）」

Check Your Comprehension

A 本文の内容について、質問に英語で答えましょう。
Answer each question in English.

1. What did Rowling use to create bedtime stories for her baby sister?
___

2. How old was Rowling when she first came up with a story about a boy wizard?
___

3. Why did Rowling return to the UK from Portugal?
___

4. How did Rowling feel after moving to Edinburgh?
___

5. Where was Rowling living when she wrote her story manuscript in 1995?
___

B 本文の内容について、質問の答えとして最も適切なものを選びましょう。
Choose the best answer for each question.

1. Why did Rowling fall into clinical depression?
   a. She had lost her imagination and ability to write.
   b. Her marriage had ended and she could not support her baby by working.
   c. She had lost her daughter due to illness.
   d. Her book had been rejected by publishing companies.

2. Why did Rowling work passionately on her book?
   a. She wanted to make money.
   b. She had nothing else to do.
   c. She wanted to forget about her miserable life.
   d. She wanted to use her manual typewriter.

3. What made it possible for Rowling to continue writing until her first book was published?
   a. Her editor's advice
   b. A grant from the Scottish Arts Council
   c. Her sister's help
   d. Welfare payments

4. What does "rock bottom" in the final sentence refer to?
   a. The time when "my greatest fear had been realized"
   b. "A positive ending"
   c. "I had an old typewriter"
   d. The time when "I was set free"

5. What does "a solid foundation on which I rebuilt my life" in the final sentence refer to?
   a. *Harry Potter and the Philosopher's Stone*
   b. The popularity of her works
   c. An £8,000 grant from the Scottish Arts Council
   d. The determination to succeed in the one area where she truly belonged

C 本文の内容と一致していれば T と、一致していなければ F と答えましょう。
Mark each sentence true (T) or false (F).

1. Rowling's mother died when the auther had just finished writing her first book. [ ]
2. Rowling separated from her husband when their daughter was about four months old. [ ]
3. Rowling wrote her story at home after her baby daughter fell asleep. [ ]
4. Rowling's manuscript was rejected by 12 publishing companies. [ ]
5. Rowling believes that her darkest hour made it possible for her to be a successful writer. [ ]

Useful Expressions from the Story

空所に本文から適切な語を補い、英文を完成させましょう。
Fill in each blank with an appropriate word from the story.

1. I _____ upon an interesting idea that night. [= thought of ~ unexpectedly]
2. I grew up on a _____ of love stories. [= reading love stories regularly]
3. He _____ up with a really creative solution. [= thought of]
4. He got _____ to studying when his brother left his room. [= began to study hard]
5. When the book _____ out, she was sure it would sell well. [= was published]

Your Thoughts on the Story

本文を読んで感じたことを、英語で書いてみましょう。必要に応じて、以下のフォーマットも活用しましょう。
Write down how you felt about the story after reading it. Use the format below if needed.

What I liked about the story is _____.

I was impressed by _____ because
_____.

After reading this story I thought _____
_____.

Story 9
A Man of Many Hats

Match the Meanings

以下の単語の意味を選びましょう。

Match each word (1~10) with the correct definition (a~j).   DL 18   CD2-02

1. accomplishment (n) [ ]
2. award (n) [ ]
3. soloist (n) [ ]
4. competitive (adj) [ ]
5. prescribe (v) [ ]
6. pregnant (adj) [ ]
7. instrument (n) [ ]
8. decline (v) [ ]
9. dialect (n) [ ]
10. credit (n) [ ]

a. trying very hard to do better than others
b. a form of a language that is spoken in one area
c. a prize for something that someone has done
d. to politely refuse to accept or to do something
e. a musician who performs alone
f. something impressive that is completed after a lot of work
g. (of a doctor) to tell someone to take a particular medicine or treatment
h. an object used to produce music
i. (of a woman) having an unborn baby developing inside her
j. praise or approval given to you because you are responsible for doing something good

Discover the Story

🎧 DL 19   💿 CD2-03 ~ 💿 CD2-09

1 By any standard, Matthias Berg is a man of many accomplishments. Since winning a national young musician award in his home country of Germany when he was only 20, Berg has become a respected French horn player. In fact, he has performed as a soloist, in a trio, in a quartet, and with orchestras all over the world, including Japan.

2 But as much as he loves music, Berg's main job is as a lawyer and a deputy district administrator for the southern state of Baden-Wurttemburg. He also just happens to be a prize-winning and highly competitive sportsman, and has been called upon to work as a sports commentator for television. After all, in the '80s and early '90s, he won a total of 27 international medals—11 golds, 10 silvers and six bronzes—in track and field and alpine skiing at the Paralympics and World Championships, making him one of the world's most decorated sports heroes.

3 Indeed, Berg's accomplishments are all the more amazing for the handicaps that life has given him. The multi-talented musician, athlete and lawyer is a victim of thalidomide, a sleeping drug that had been prescribed to some 7,000 women around the world in the late '50s and early '60s. Much later, it was discovered that when taken between the 21st and 36th day of a pregnancy, at a time when some women would not even realize they were pregnant, thalidomide can severely affect the unborn child. Berg was born in 1961 with very short arms and two fingers missing on each hand.

4 Berg came from a musical family. His mother had studied the organ, his father was a music teacher, his sister is a mezzo-soprano, and his brother is a professional percussionist. With such talent in the family, there was no question that music would play a role in his life, too.

5 "My handicap limited the choice of instruments. So really, only the French horn could be considered. It only needs three fingers for the valves, and you can rest it on your lap when you are sitting down. Additionally, it helps that although I am right-handed, my left hand had been trained in my younger years, and the valves of the French horn are usually

played on the left. My parents thought it was the ideal instrument—it required musicality but also encouraged physical development. And I didn't really want to learn the pan pipes," said Berg in an interview with *Klassik Magazin*, a publication about classical music. Berg was even offered a permanent place with an orchestra, which he declined in favor of law studies.

6 When he was 10, Berg's family moved from the north of Germany to Stuttgart in the south. "Did the kids make fun of you because of your handicap?" asked an interviewer on a television program. Berg replied, "Yes, but I was already strange because of my accent. Stuttgart has a very special dialect!"

7 Today, besides performing regularly and commenting on sports, Berg also gives motivational speeches in matters related to music, sports, law and physical disabilities. It seems that this amazing man is only adding one more line to an already excellent list of career credits.

Notes | **trio**「三重奏」 **quartet**「四重奏」 **deputy district administrator**「州副知事、地区副行政官」 **thalidomide**「サリドマイド」鎮痛薬、催眠薬 **mezzo-soprano**「メゾソプラノ歌手」 **percussionist**「打楽器（パーカッション）奏者」 **valve**「（金管楽器の）ピストン、バルブ」 **pan pipes**「パンパイプ」アシなどの長短の管を並べた原始的な笛

Check Your Comprehension

A 本文の内容について、質問に英語で答えましょう。
Answer each question in English.

1. What instrument does Berg play?

2. In what sports has Berg won international medals?

3. How many jobs does Berg have?

4. What is Berg's handicap?

5. What does Berg do these days in addition to his regular jobs?

B 本文の内容について、質問の答えとして最も適切なものを選びましょう。
Choose the best answer for each question.

1. What caused Berg to have handicaps?
   a. He had a traffic accident when he was a baby.
   b. His mother took a sleeping drug when she was pregnant.
   c. His mother had a traffic accident when she was pregnant.
   d. He got injured in his childhood when he was skiing.

2. What does "the world's most decorated sports heroes" in the 2nd paragraph mean?
   a. The sports heroes who wear colorful uniforms
   b. The sports heroes who won medals in two different sports
   c. The sports heroes who won different colors of medals
   d. The sports heroes who paint different colors on their faces

3. How did Berg choose the instrument he plays?
   a. He liked the sound of the instrument.
   b. His friend played the same instrument.
   c. The instrument was ideal for his physical condition.
   d. His brother wanted him to play the instrument.

4. Why did Berg decline the job offer of a permanent place with an orchestra?
   a. He liked studying law.
   b. He liked skiing.
   c. He liked working as a deputy district administrator.
   d. He liked having free time.

5. What doesn't Berg talk about in his speeches?
   a. Law
   b. Music
   c. Medicine
   d. Physical disabilities

C 本文の内容と一致していれば T と、一致していなければ F と答えましょう。
Mark each sentence true (T) or false (F).

1. Berg plays the French horn only when he performs with orchestras. [ ]
2. One of Berg's parents was a music teacher. [ ]
3. Berg has won more than ten gold medals. [ ]
4. Berg wanted to play the pan pipes, but gave up the idea because of his handicap. [ ]
5. Berg is too busy to work as a commentator these days. [ ]

Useful Expressions from the Story

空所に本文から適切な語を補い、英文を完成させましょう。
Fill in each blank with an appropriate word from the story.

1. The governor _____ upon everyone to save water. [= asked]
2. There is no _____ that Mary drew this picture. [= It is clear]
3. He gave up studying history in _____ of economics. [= preferring]
4. Tom often makes _____ of his little sister. [= laughs at]
5. She talked about a topic _____ to sports. [= connected with]

Your Thoughts on the Story

本文を読んで感じたことを、英語で書いてみましょう。必要に応じて、以下のフォーマットも活用しましょう。
Write down how you felt about the story after reading it. Use the format below if needed.

What I liked about the story is _____.

I was impressed by _____ because
_____.

After reading this story I thought _____
_____
_____.

Story 10

Jiri's Legacy

Match the Meanings

以下の単語の意味を選びましょう。

Match each word (1~10) with the correct definition (a~j). DL 20 CD2-10

1. disability (n)   [   ]
2. outlive (v)   [   ]
3. founder (n)   [   ]
4. facility (n)   [   ]
5. trainee (n)   [   ]
6. skeptical (adj) [   ]
7. launch (n)   [   ]
8. resolve (n)   [   ]
9. legacy (n)   [   ]
10. empower (v)   [   ]

a. a person who starts an organization or a business
b. starting an organized project or activity
c. to continue to exist after something else has ended or disappeared
d. to give someone more control over their own actions in life or in a situation
e. tending to doubt what others tell you
f. firm determination to do something
g. a condition of being unable to use a part of your body because of an illness, injury, etc.
h. a person who is training for a particular job
i. a place used for a particular purpose or activity
j. a situation that exists now because of events, activities, etc. that took place before

Discover the Story

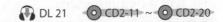

1 If you ask someone in Zimbabwe to name a rehabilitation center, chances are good that the first organization they will mention is the Jairos Jiri Association—an organization that is known for rehabilitation programs for people with disabilities.

2 However, should you ask further about the history behind the name, heads are likely to be scratched, and fewer people will be able to give a satisfying answer. This is understandable, as not only has the organization outlived its founder Jairos Jiri himself, but it was also more well known than the face behind the name, even during his lifetime.

3 Jairos Jiri was born in 1921, a time when Zimbabwe was still under colonial rule with a government that did not support the education of black people. He only received primary school education, and took care of the family cattle until the age of 12. Later, he supported himself by caring for other people's goats, washing dishes in the army and working at a bottle store.

4 Despite his limited education, Jiri was moved by the problems of people with disabilities and started to do something about it after World War II. To show that blind people could be taught to help themselves, he raised money by arranging for a blind band to play to African audiences. He also sold newspapers in the mornings and soft drinks at weekend sporting events as another way to raise additional funds.

5 Recognizing Jiri's efforts, the local government soon gave him a room in the highly crowded suburbs on a three-month test period. The room was his association's first facility, and its first trainee was Josef Ncube. At first, Josef was skeptical since he was used to begging and did not see the sense in what Jiri had proposed. That was when Jiri made the famous statement: "Our experience is, so long as they [the blind] have hands, they are able to do something."

6 With more people being brought in, Jairos Jiri stated that the organization was based on Christian principles of charity, patience and non-judgmental tolerance. Yet all the odds were stacked against him. He started the organization at a time when there was segregation, with black people being viewed as second-class citizens. Moreover, lack of funding was a great challenge, since there were no philanthropic organizations founded by black people at that time.

7 About a decade after its launch, however, the Jairos Jiri Association was able to receive a government grant in order to open an art center. It became a hit with tourists because of the beautiful art objects it sold—and continues to sell more than half a century later.

8 The success of the organization was the result of Jairos Jiri's resolve to succeed, so it is not surprising that the legacy lives on. Apart from the art center, the organization also began promoting other rehabilitation projects, including carpentry, wall plaque making, carving, pottery, painting and sculpture. This gave hope to people with disabilities in the region, empowering them through skills training. Within a short time, each town in Zimbabwe had a Jairos Jiri branch, where the trademark art objects, baskets and woven products are always on display.

9 Jairos Jiri died in 1982, but his legacy continues through his organization. At one time, its music program even produced one of the leading music groups in the country, called the Jairos Jiri Band, whose lead singer was a blind social worker.

10 With limited education and simple beginnings, Jairos Jiri has been able to change the lives of a great number of people. He was a special individual that made a difference.

Notes | **rehabilitation**「リハビリテーション」社会復帰のための技能、職能訓練
non-judgmental tolerance「個人的な基準によらない寛容」　**segregation**「人種差別（分離、隔絶）」　**philanthropic**「博愛（主義）の、慈善（事業）の」　**carpentry**「木工」　**wall plaque making**「飾り板製作」　**carving**「木彫り、象牙彫り」　**pottery**「陶器製造」

Check Your Comprehension

A 本文の内容について、質問に英語で答えましょう。
Answer each question in English.

1. What is the Jairos Jiri Association?

2. Why did Jairos Jiri arrange for a blind band to play to African audiences to raise money?

3. What principles was the Jairos Jiri Association based on?

4. What challenges did Jairos Jiri face when he started the organization?

5. Why was Jairos Jiri a special person?

B 本文の内容について、質問の答えとして最も適切なものを選びましょう。
Choose the best answer for each question.

1. What does "the face behind the name" in the 2nd paragraph mean?
   a. The plate of a clock with the name
   b. The history of the name
   c. The person who had the name
   d. The person who found the name

2. How did Jairos Jiri get a place that was the first facility of his association?
   a. His friends helped him to get it.
   b. The local government gave it to him as an experiment.
   c. The blind people in his area provided it to him.
   d. The people in his church rented it for him to use.

3. What does "all the odds were stacked against him" in the 6th paragraph mean?
   a. Jiri had great difficulty in running the organization.
   b. All the staff of the organization often disagreed with Jiri's ideas.
   c. Things didn't go as well as Jiri had expected because of Christian principles.
   d. Because there were great challenges, he gave up running the organization.

4. What was it that led the organization to success?
   a. Jairos Jiri's music talent
   b. Jairos Jiri's skills to raise cattle
   c. Jairos Jiri's creativity to produce art objects
   d. Jairos Jiri's determination to succeed

5. What is Jairos Jiri's legacy?
   a. The school and hospital that the organization founded
   b. The park the organization created
   c. The art center and rehabilitation projects, such as carpentry and carving
   d. The hall where the music groups perform

C 本文の内容と一致していればTと、一致していなければFと答えましょう。
Mark each sentence true (T) or false (F).

1. The Jairos Jiri Association is a famous rehabilitation center in Zimbabwe. [   ]
2. Jairos Jiri went to high school but soon left to support his family. [   ]
3. Josef immediately knew that Jiri was proposing the right thing. [   ]
4. Jiri became the first black person to start a philanthropic organization in Zimbabwe. [   ]
5. The Jairos Jiri Band was managed by Jairos Jiri. [   ]

Useful Expressions from the Story

空所に本文から適切な語を補い、英文を完成させましょう。
Fill in each blank with an appropriate word from the story.

1. _____ you ask about their country's history, they will answer easily. [= If you should ask]
2. Heads are likely to be _____. [= People are likely to find it difficult to answer]
3. I know they can _____ themselves. [= make efforts without depending on others]
4. _____ more people being brought in, the project was finished quickly. [= When more people were brought in]
5. He is a special individual that _____ a difference to people's lives. [= changed people's lives]

Your Thoughts on the Story

本文を読んで感じたことを、英語で書いてみましょう。必要に応じて、以下のフォーマットも活用しましょう。
Write down how you felt about the story after reading it. Use the format below if needed.

What I liked about the story is _____.

I was impressed by _____ because
_____.

After reading this story I thought _____
_____.

Story 11

From Rags to Riches

Match the Meanings

以下の単語の意味を選びましょう。

Match each word or phrase (1~10) with the correct definition (a~j).

DL 22   CD2-21

1. flee (v)   [   ]
2. sibling (n)   [   ]
3. setback (n)   [   ]
4. landlord (n)   [   ]
5. purchase (n)   [   ]
6. real estate (n)   [   ]
7. property (n)   [   ]
8. debt (n)   [   ]
9. capital (n)   [   ]
10. insight (n)   [   ]

a. houses, buildings, or land that are bought and sold
b. sum of money you owe
c. a brother or sister
d. a difficulty or problem that prevents something from happening or progressing
e. to escape from a dangerous place or situation
f. a person or company who rents a room or building to someone
g. the act of buying something
h. land and buildings that are owned by someone
i. the ability to see and understand the truth about people or situations
j. a large amount of money that is invested to start a business or to produce more wealth

Discover the Story

1 Li Ka-Shing was born on June 13, 1928 in the southeastern coastal city of Chiuchow, China. Although his father was the principal of a primary school in Guangdong province, Li had little opportunity for formal education due to political problems in the country during his youth.

2 His schooling was interrupted when his family fled to Hong Kong from mainland China in 1940 to escape the Japanese invasion. At the age of 15, his father passed away from overwork, leaving Li to carry on the burden of supporting his mother and three younger siblings.

3 However, the young man did not let this setback stop him from moving forward with his life. He immediately left school and took on a job selling watchbands for his uncle. When Li was 17, he moved on to work as a salesman for a hardware factory. His hard work and intelligence earned him the respect of his bosses, and within a year, he was promoted to the position of Department Manager, and after that, General Manager when he was barely 20 years old.

4 Li's talents enabled him to start his own plastics factory in a rented building in 1950. During the first ten years, the hardworking Li worked 16-hour days, seven days a week, manufacturing plastic toys and household products that were shipped to Europe and America. Despite the tough schedule, Li never lost his passion for education, often staying up late to study. Moreover, surviving on only two hours of sleep each night, Li never missed a day of work unless he was sick.

5 His hard work paid off, and by 1957 Li had a strong business that was ready to expand. By 1958, he had carefully saved US$7,000, so when the landlord of his factory tried to raise the rent, Li used his savings to buy the building.

6 This purchase would be the first of Li's many investments in real estate. By the 1960s, his company, Cheung Kong Industries, had been transformed into a property development and management company, becoming one of the top five real estate companies in Hong Kong.

7 Li's money-saving ways showed in his business strategy: he avoided debt by raising capital before building, doing so via joint ventures with landowners or by selling apartments in advance to friends and colleagues. This made his investments less risky while still earning profits for both Li and his co-investors. His company grew rapidly and had its initial public offering in 1972. Seven years on, Li was Hong Kong's largest private landlord.

8 Through Li's hard work and sharp business insights, Cheung Kong Holdings entered into other industries such as ports, telecommunications, finance, infrastructure and biotechnology. However, despite his great success, Li never forgets to give back to society, and has contributed more than US$1.27 billion to philanthropic causes so far.

9 As Li once said to the people of Hong Kong, "The future may be made up of many factors, but where it truly lies is in the hearts and minds of individuals. Your dedication should not be kept for your own gain, but [you should] unleash your passion for our beloved country as well as for the sincerity and humanity of mankind." Today, he is one of the wealthiest men in East Asia, and his various holdings employ over 260,000 people worldwide.

Notes **Chiuchow**「中国潮州市」 **Guangdong province**「広東省」 **burden**「重荷、負担、責任」 **investment**「投資」 **initial public offering**「最初の株式や債券の公募」 **holdings**「持株会社所有の会社」 **cause**「主義、(主義のために活動する) 団体」 **dedication**「献身、専念」 **unleash**「〜を解き放つ」 **sincerity**「誠実、誠意」

Check Your Comprehension

A 本文の内容について、質問に英語で答えましょう。
Answer each question in English.

1. Why did Li's family flee to Hong Kong from mainland China?

2. What did Li do when his father passed away?

3. Why was Li able to get promoted to high positions quickly?

4. What was Li's business strategy?

5. What industries does Cheung Kong Holdings include today?

B 本文の内容について、質問の答えとして最も適切なものを選びましょう。
Choose the best answer for each question.

1. What does "this setback" in the 3rd paragraph mean?
   a. Li's family moved to Hong Kong from mainland China.
   b. Li had three younger siblings.
   c. Li's father died from overwork.
   d. Li's mother was sick in bed.

2. What was Li's first job?
   a. Selling watchbands
   b. Producing plastics
   c. Selling factory tools and equipment
   d. Buying land and houses

3. How old was Li when he owned his factory?
   a. 17 years old
   b. 22 years old
   c. 32 years old
   d. 37 years old

4. What does "this purchase" in the 6th paragraph mean?
   a. Li bought the factory that he had rented for several years.
   b. Li bought a property development company.
   c. Li bought apartments for his family members.
   d. Li bought a hardware factory for which he had worked as a salesman.

5. Li states: "The future may be made up of many factors, but where it truly lies is in the hearts and minds of individuals." What does he think is important for people to do for a better future?
   a. We should work hard to support our family.
   b. We should study hard to gain new insight.
   c. We should save money for our future success.
   d. We should contribute to society.

C

本文の内容と一致していれば T と、一致していなければ F と答えましょう。
Mark each sentence true (T) or false (F).

1. Li didn't receive much formal education. [ ]
2. Li worked so hard that he could barely study despite his passion for education. [ ]
3. Li worked hard every day with only two hours of sleep. [ ]
4. Li started to expand his business through investing in real estate. [ ]
5. Li is concerned about his country but not about the humanity of mankind. [ ]

Useful Expressions from the Story

空所に本文から適切な語を補い、英文を完成させましょう。
Fill in each blank with an appropriate word from the story.

1. Tom _____ up late to study. [= studied until late at night]
2. My efforts _____ off. [= had the result that was intended]
3. Her company was _____ into a management company. [= was completely changed]
4. I'll let you know my flight number in _____. [= before an action or event]
5. We _____ into this activity last year. [= became involved in]

Your Thoughts on the Story

本文を読んで感じたことを、英語で書いてみましょう。必要に応じて、以下のフォーマットも活用しましょう。
Write down how you felt about the story after reading it. Use the format below if needed.

What I liked about the story is _____.

I was impressed by _____ because _____.

After reading this story I thought _____.

Story 12
Priceless Courage

Match the Meanings

以下の単語の意味を選びましょう。
Match each word (1~10) with the correct definition (a~j). DL 24   CD2-31

1. staff (v)   [   ]   **a.** a famous person; a star
2. compensation (n)   [   ]   **b.** to hold and keep something or someone from
3. equipment (n)   [   ]   falling
4. hesitation (n)   [   ]   **c.** cheerfully; happily
5. lean (v)   [   ]   **d.** not covered with any clothing
6. bare (adj)   [   ]   **e.** a person who has the power to make laws
7. steady (v)   [   ]   **f.** to provide workers for a company, etc.
8. lightheartedly (adv) [   ]   **g.** tools and machines used for work
9. celebrity (n)   [   ]   **h.** a pause or delay before saying or doing
10. legislator (n)   [   ]   something
                                i. to put an object on or against something in a
                                    sloping position
                                j. money given to someone because they have
                                    been hurt or because something they own
                                    has been damaged

Discover the Story

1 While the fire departments in most American cities are staffed by paid professional firefighters, most suburban communities are protected by volunteer fire departments. The men and women volunteers are often called upon to risk their lives, while receiving no pay or compensation other than the good feeling one gets when helping others.

2 One such man is John Curley, a career firefighter with the New York City Fire Department, who has also served his local Bellmore Fire Department as a volunteer for almost 30 years. He showed his bravery when he rescued a 93-year-old woman from a burning house in November 2012.

3 That day, Curley was helping neighbors who were still without heat because of the damage done recently by Hurricane Sandy. He and his son were on their way to get new heating equipment when he heard an emergency call on his radio saying that a two-story house was on fire. Without hesitation, Curley rushed to help without the gloves, protective clothing or tools he normally uses when responding to a fire call.

4 At the burning house, a 61-year-old man who was covered with black soot said his mother was still in the house, in a second-floor bedroom. Curley and his son set a ladder on top of a filing cabinet and leaned it against the house. Curley then climbed to the window and broke it with his bare hands.

5 Curley could see an elderly woman lying on the floor, obviously overcome by the thick smoke. The door was already starting to burn off the hinges, and fire was coming through the walls. Even though he had burned his hands, and his face and scalp were cut from the hot glass, Curley went inside, picked up the woman and took her to the window. Holding her in his arms, he carried her down the ladder just in time. At that very moment, the bedroom went up in flames.

6 Luckily, by the time Curley had brought the woman to the window, firefighters and police officers were at the scene. They steadied the ladder while he climbed down and they received the woman from Curley.

7 The house was in an area severely damaged by Hurricane Sandy, and the only heat available came from an electric heater. Fire officials are not sure if that is what caused the fire, but whatever the cause, there is no doubt that the woman would have died if Curley had not risked his life to save her.

8 "I broke the window with my bare hands—not recommended," Curley recalled lightheartedly when interviewed immediately after the incident. He added, "I feel good. When you save a life, that's great."

⑨ Neighbors were quick to praise their hero. A fire officer on the scene of the fire agreed: "It was heroic. He did a great job." Local newspapers praised Curley, and the neighbors were proud of their local celebrity. Moreover, in a show of appreciation, he was honored by the Nassau County Legislature, receiving their Good Samaritan Award and even more publicity.

⑩ The legislator presenting the award said, "I think that all of us know that our fire department put their lives on the line to protect us. Even as volunteers, John Curley and his son went above and beyond the call of duty. They were heroes and literally saved the life of a complete stranger. That is what our firemen and women do, day in and day out."

Notes | **Hurricane Sandy**「ハリケーン・サンディ」2012 年に発生したハリケーンの一つで、多大な被害を及ぼした。ニューヨーク市では広範囲で浸水に見舞われ、停電も多発した。　**soot**「すす、煤煙」　　**hinge**「(開き戸などの) ちょうつがい」　　**scalp**「頭皮」　**Nassau County Legislature**「ナッソー郡議会」ナッソー郡はニューヨーク市の東に隣接　**Good Samaritan Award**「善きサマリア人賞」人種・信条・肌の色に関係なく、悩み苦しむ人を無私に助けた人に与えられる賞。"Good Samaritan" は聖書に由来し『困っている人に親切な人』の意味

Check Your Comprehension

 本文の内容について、質問に英語で答えましょう。
Answer each question in English.

1. What do volunteer firefighters receive by risking their lives when called upon?

2. What were Curley and his son doing when they heard an emergency call on the radio?

3. How did Curley get into the burning house?

4. What had happened to Curley's body when he went to pick up the elderly woman?

5. How was Curley treated after he saved the elderly woman?

B 本文の内容について、質問の答えとして最も適切なものを選びましょう。
Choose the best answer for each question.

1. Where does Curley serve as a firefighter?
   a. The New York City Fire Department
   b. The Bellmore Fire Department
   c. The Nassau County Fire Department and Bellmore Fire Department
   d. The New York City Fire Department and Bellmore Fire Department

2. How many people were in the burning house when Curly arrived?
   a. Four people
   b. Three people
   c. Two people
   d. One person

3. What did the other firefighters do when they arrived at the scene?
   a. They carried the old woman with Curley.
   b. They helped Curley climb down the ladder.
   c. They threw a rope for Curley to hold.
   d. They called an ambulance.

4. Why was an electric heater the only source of heating in the house that was on fire?
   a. The house was in an underdeveloped area.
   b. The house was near a building under construction.
   c. The house was in an area damaged by a recent hurricane.
   d. The house was in an area damaged by a recent earthquake.

5. What does "their local celebrity" in the 9th paragraph refer to?
   a. Curley
   b. Curley and his son
   c. Curley and his fellow firefighters
   d. Curley and the fire officers at the scene

Story 12 | Priceless Courage

C 本文の内容と一致していれば T と、一致していなければ F と答えましょう。
Mark each sentence true (T) or false (F).

1. Every US firefighter is not paid by their city or local community. [ ]
2. Before Curley carried the woman out of the house, other firefighters had arrived at the scene. [ ]
3. The cause of the fire was found to be an electric heater used in the house. [ ]
4. In fire situations, Curley recommends breaking windows with bare hands. [ ]
5. The legislator said that not all the firefighters were as heroic as Curley. [ ]

Useful Expressions from the Story

空所に本文から適切な語を補い、英文を完成させましょう。
Fill in each blank with an appropriate word from the story.

1. The moment he came out, the house <u>went up in</u> _____. [= was destroyed by fire]
2. The only room _____ was the one next to hers. [= that they could use]
3. The girl _____ have failed if he had not helped her. [= didn't fail because he helped]
4. John put his future <u>on the</u> _____ to help us. [= at serious risk]
5. Mary <u>went above and beyond the</u> _____ <u>of duty</u>. [= did more than what she had to do]

Your Thoughts on the Story

本文を読んで感じたことを、英語で書いてみましょう。必要に応じて、以下のフォーマットも活用しましょう。
Write down how you felt about the story after reading it. Use the format below if needed.

What I liked about the story is _____.

I was impressed by _____ because
_____.

After reading this story I thought _____
_____.

Story 13

Another Battle

Match the Meanings

以下の単語の意味を選びましょう。

Match each word (1~10) with the correct definition (a~j). DL 26 CD2-42

1. inscribe (v) [ ]
2. aircraft (n) [ ]
3. cargo (n) [ ]
4. burn (n) [ ]
5. undergo (v) [ ]
6. suicidal (adj) [ ]
7. goodwill (n) [ ]
8. patron (n) [ ]
9. disfigurement (n) [ ]
10. tribute (n) [ ]

a. to write, print or carve words, names, etc. onto something

b. the goods that are carried on a ship or plane

c. the appearance of a person or thing which causes it to lose its beauty or value

d. an act or statement that is intended to show your respect or admiration

e. an injury or damage caused by fire, heat, or acid

f. a famous or important person who supports an organization such as a charity

g. friendly or helpful feelings towards others

h. a machine that is able to fly and carry goods or passengers

i. deeply unhappy and depressed and likely to kill yourself

j. to experience something, usually unpleasant

Discover the Story

1 In 2012, Simon Weston and his family went on a journey to the Falkland Islands, located in the South Atlantic Ocean, nearly 500 km from the South American mainland. Here, 30 years before, a war had been fought between Britain and Argentina over ownership of the islands. Standing in front of a memorial with the names of the soldiers who had fallen in that conflict, Weston thought about how close his own name had come to being inscribed on it.

2 On June 9, 1982, Weston, then a soldier in the Welsh Guards, was on Sir Galahad, an unarmed transport ship carrying men and supplies to the Falklands. Suddenly, Argentinean aircraft attacked the ship, and since much of its cargo was fuel and bullets, it quickly caught fire.

3 That day, the Welsh Guards lost 48 men aboard the ship and many more were left injured. Among Weston's team of 30 men, only eight survived the attack. Weston himself suffered burns over 46 percent of his body. In fact, he was so badly burned that when he was sent back to Britain and his mother and grandmother saw him for the first time, they did not recognize him until he spoke.

4 Over the following years, Weston underwent several painful operations to repair some of the damage to his face and body. Those were the low points of his career. "I spent a lot of time locking myself away in my bedroom and drinking huge amounts of alcohol," he said in a television interview in 2006. "There must be people living now as I did. I wasn't living—I was existing. I became suicidal and almost took my own life."

5 However, Weston got through this dark period with the support of his mother, who contacted his former regiment. She asked the soldiers to encourage her son to be positive and think of his future, which they did. With such love and encouragement, he moved toward a brighter path in his life.

6 Then, in 1986 Weston was invited to Australia to take a goodwill tour around the country. While there, the amount of money he raised for children's burn units persuaded him that he could be influential and useful in this field. Subsequently, he became a patron of many charities that help people with disfigurements such as his own, and in 1988, set up his own youth charity, Weston Spirit. Sadly, it had to close because of financial difficulties 20 years later, but it was there that he met and married Lucy, a worker for the charity.

7 Weston's courage and charity work have been recognized many times. He was awarded the Freedom of the City of Liverpool and given a high honor from the Queen and an Honorary Fellowship of Cardiff University. He has also campaigned on behalf of soldiers, speaking out against defense cuts, and servicemen not being given enough equipment. Importantly, he spoke about the treatment given to former soldiers, especially those injured while on duty.

8 Weston became a well-known personality on radio and television and has written several novels and autobiographies. Perhaps the best tribute to him was given by the website "100 Welsh Heroes." It reads: "He sets a supreme example of how to take whatever setbacks life has in store for you. Unlike most brave soldiers, Simon Weston's heroism did not begin until his army days were done."

Notes | **the Falkland Islands**「フォークランド諸島」南大西洋上にあるイギリス領の諸島で、1833年からイギリスが実効支配を続け、現在に至る **the Welsh Guards**「ウェールズ近衛連隊」イギリス近衛師団の一つで、イギリス軍の歩兵連隊 **regiment**「連隊」 **high honor**「栄誉賞」 **Honorary Fellowship of Cardiff University**「カーディフ大学名誉フェロー」名誉フェローは学術称号で特別研究員の地位 **defense cut**「防衛費削減」 **serviceman**「軍人」 **autobiography**「自叙伝」

Check Your Comprehension

A 本文の内容について、質問に英語で答えましょう。
Answer each question in English.

1. What happened to Weston when the ship he was aboard was attacked on June 9, 1982?

2. Why did Weston go through painful operations?

3. How did Weston get through this difficult time in his life?

4. What happened to make Weston think that he could help people with disfigurements like his own?

5. What is considered the best tribute given to Weston?

B 本文の内容について、質問の答えとして最も適切なものを選びましょう。
Choose the best answer for each question.

1. What was "Sir Galahad"?
   a. An aircraft that was transporting soldiers and supplies
   b. A ship which was transporting soldiers and supplies
   c. An aircraft that attacked the enemy with weapons
   d. A ship that attacked the enemy with weapons

2. How badly was Weston burned?
   a. He suffered burns over half of his body.
   b. He was burned so badly that he completely lost his voice.
   c. He suffered burns over two thirds of his body.
   d. He was burned so badly that his family recognized him only after he spoke.

3. What does "the low points of his career" in the 4th paragraph mean?
   a. The time when Weston was unhappy and depressed
   b. The days when Weston was ranked in a low position
   c. The time when Weston was regarded as poor by his fellow soldiers
   d. The time when Weston was kept in bed because of his illness

4. What did Weston start after his trip to Australia?
   a. Supporting young soldiers
   b. Speaking on behalf of soldiers
   c. Supporting charities and establishing his own charity
   d. Appearing on radio and television

5. What does "Simon Weston's heroism" in the 8th paragraph mean?
   a. Weston's high honor given from the Queen
   b. Weston's goodwill tour around Australia
   c. Weston's honorary Fellowship of Cardiff University
   d. Weston's courage and charity work

C 本文の内容と一致していればTと、一致していなければFと答えましょう。
Mark each sentence true (T) or false (F).

1. Simon Weston fought in the war between Britain and Germany. [ ]
2. Weston's name is inscribed on a memorial on the Falkland Islands. [ ]
3. Weston was successful in raising money for children's burn units in 1986. [ ]
4. Through his charity work Weston met a woman who became his wife. [ ]
5. Weston is famous not only for his charity work but for his campaign on behalf of soldiers. [ ]

Useful Expressions from the Story

空所に本文から適切な語を補い、英文を完成させましょう。
Fill in each blank with an appropriate word from the story.

1. She _____ close to being hit by a car. [= was almost]
2. The woman almost _____ her own life. [= killed herself]
3. My father _____ my teacher and asked her to help me. [= got in touch with]
4. He _____ up his own charity last year. [= started]
5. I've got a surprise in _____ for you. [= waiting for]

Your Thoughts on the Story

本文を読んで感じたことを、英語で書いてみましょう。必要に応じて、以下のフォーマットも活用しましょう。
Write down how you felt about the story after reading it. Use the format below if needed.

What I liked about the story is _____.

I was impressed by _____ because
_____.

Also, I felt that _____
_____.

After reading this story I thought _____
_____.

Story 14

Nehanda's Bones

Match the Meanings

以下の単語の意味を選びましょう。

Match each word or phrase (1~10) with the correct definition (a~j).

DL 28　　CD2-51

1. occupy (v)　　[　]
2. fertile (adj)　　[　]
3. independence (n)　　[　]
4. make a prediction (v)
5. mobilize (v)　　[　]
6. ancestor (n)　　[　]
7. invader (n)　　[　]
8. commander (n)　　[　]
9. capture (v)　　[　]
10. sentence (v)　　[　]

a. to say that something will happen in the future
b. to catch a person and keep them as a prisoner
c. an army, a group of soldiers or a country that enters another country or area by force
d. an officer who is in charge of a group of soldiers
e. a member in a family who lived a long time ago
f. to enter a place in a large group or army and take control of it by force
g. to organize a group or people to achieve a particular aim
h. freedom from political control by the government or other countries
i. of land or soil that plants grow well in
j. to state in court that someone is to receive a particular punishment

Discover the Story

1 Walking in Harare, Zimbabwe's capital, one will notice that the name Nehanda is part of everyday life in this city: it is given to roads, training institutions, hospital wards and even a netball team. Clearly, it belongs to a very special and popular person, but who is Nehanda?

2 While Harare's major roads are named after heroes who participated in the war of liberation, fought between 1966 and 1980, Nehanda is a heroine who lived almost 70 years before the start of this war.

3 When the British occupied what is now modern-day Zimbabwe in 1890, they pushed the African people away from the fertile land. In addition, the British took cattle from the locals, made them pay taxes and introduced forced labor.

4 Unfortunately, the Africans could not organize themselves to fight against the colonizers. The main reason for this was that their society consisted of many tribes with very small or no armies at all, and they could not face the firepower of the British colonizers, who were better organized.

5 In 1896, the Africans faced serious problems when rinderpest, a rare cattle disease, attacked the few cattle they were left with. Cattle played a central role in the African economy as a store of wealth and a source of meat, milk and other animal products.

6 The disease also played an important role in the fight for independence, which was strongly influenced by one particular woman. Nehanda, a spiritual leader of the Shona people, was living less than 50 kilometers north of Harare. Her role was to make predictions and perform traditional ceremonies to pray for rain and good harvests.

7 Although Nehanda had initially tried to maintain a friendly relationship with the Europeans, the problems of the locals were too much to bear. She finally mobilized the people, saying their ancestors wanted them to drive away the invaders and doing so would bring an end to rinderpest. She started sending messengers to chiefs across Zimbabwe, encouraging them to rise up against the colonizers. The mobilization was done so quietly that the British were caught by surprise when they were attacked by the Shona people, whom they considered to be very peaceful.

8 Nehanda was the commander in the war that lasted slightly more than a year. Her strategies, especially taking the enemy by surprise, made the difference in a war where Africa faced the very advanced weapons of the British. So important was her role that, in 1897, the British captured her, together with Kaguvi, another religious leader, and sentenced them to death. It is said that before Nehanda died, she said, "My bones will rise again" to lead another struggle against the Europeans.

9 When the Africans started fighting for liberation again in 1966, their political leaders made reference to Nehanda's last words, saying the freedom fighters were her "bones"—and this time, after a guerilla war that lasted for 14 years, Zimbabwe finally gained independence. It is for this reason that more than 100 years after her death, Nehanda is still considered the "grandmother" of Zimbabwe.

Notes **Harare**「ハラレ」アフリカ大陸南部のジンバブエ共和国の首都で、この国最大の都市　**hospital ward**「病棟」　**netball**「ネットボール」1チーム7人で行うバスケットボールに似た球技　**colonizer**「植民地開拓者」　**tribe**「種族、部族」　**rinderpest**「牛疫」ウイルスによるウシ・ヒツジなど偶蹄類の悪性の伝染病　**guerilla war**「ゲリラ戦」奇襲によって、敵を混乱させ、敵が集中的威力を発揮する前に姿を消して打撃を逃れる戦法

Check Your Comprehension

A 本文の内容について、質問に英語で答えましょう。
Answer each question in English.

1. What did the British do in 1890 to the people in what is now modern-day Zimbabwe?

2. Why couldn't African people organize themselves to fight against the British?

3. Why did Nehanda stop trying to maintain a friendly relationship with the Europeans?

4. How did Nehanda mobilize African people in order to fight against the Europeans?

5. Why is Nehanda still considered the "grandmother" of Zimbabwe today?

B 本文の内容について、質問の答えとして最も適切なものを選びましょう。
Choose the best answer for each question.

1. Which places in Zimbabwe have the name Nehanda?
   a. All the hospitals in the country
   b. Many mountains and rivers all over the country
   c. Many things in everyday life in the capital city
   d. Many villages in Zimbabwe

2. Why was rinderpest such a big problem for Africans?
   a. The disease killed the animals that were important for their lives.
   b. The disease killed not only animals but also people.
   c. The disease caused the plants to die, which led to animal deaths.
   d. The disease killed the woman who played an important role for African people.

3. What was Nehanda's job?
   a. To lead people in the fight against other tribes
   b. To teach people how to maintain good health
   c. To take care of sick people and pray for the Shona people
   d. To tell people about future happenings and pray for rain and good harvests

4. What strategy did Nehanda take in the war against the British, who used advanced weapons?
   a. Firepower
   b. A surprise attack
   c. Poison
   d. Magic words

5. What did her message "My bones will rise again" mean?
   a. My spirit will return in the fight for independence.
   b. My bones will stand up one more time.
   c. My grave will be built in the future.
   d. My bones will not disappear.

C 本文の内容と一致していればTと、一致していなければFと答えましょう。
Mark each sentence true (T) or false (F).

1. It is clear that the name Nehanda is popular in Harare. [ ]
2. Nehanda is a woman who fought between 1966 and 1980. [ ]
3. Nehanda told people that fighting against the French would end rinderpest. [ ]
4. Nehanda was such an important leader that the British decided to release her. [ ]
5. Zimbabwe won the war after a long fight in which soldiers were encouraged by Nehanda's last words. [ ]

Useful Expressions from the Story

空所に本文から適切な語を補い、英文を完成させましょう。
Fill in each blank with an appropriate word from the story.

1. Those heroes _____ in the war of liberation. [= took part in]
2. Your actions will _____ an end to the disease. [= end]
3. The news <u>caught him</u> _____ surprise. [= attacked him unexpectedly]
4. _____ sad was Mary that she started to cry. [= Mary was very sad, so]
5. They <u>made</u> _____ <u>to</u> the famous person's words. [= spoke about]

Your Thoughts on the Story

本文を読んで感じたことを、英語で書いてみましょう。必要に応じて、以下のフォーマットも活用しましょう。
Write down how you felt about the story after reading it. Use the format below if needed.

What I liked about the story is _____.

I was impressed by _____ because

_____.

Also, I felt that _____

_____.

After reading this story I thought _____

_____.

Story 15

A Trickle Effect

Match the Meanings

以下の単語の意味を選びましょう。

Match each word (1~10) with the correct definition (a~j).　DL 30　CD2-61

1. diverse (adj)　[ ]
2. intolerance (n)　[ ]
3. innocent (adj)　[ ]
4. interfaith (adj)　[ ]
5. worship (n)　[ ]
6. ethnicity (n)　[ ]
7. discrimination (n)　[ ]
8. transcend (v)　[ ]
9. compassion (n)　[ ]
10. trickle (n)　[ ]

a. a small amount of something that moves slowly
b. being injured or killed as a result of a crime or conflict although not directly involved in it
c. an act of expressing respect for a god
d. between or relating to different religions
e. to go beyond the normal limits or boundaries
f. being made up of a wide variety
g. unwillingness to accept different opinions or people
h. treating a particular group less fairly than others
i. a feeling of sympathy and understanding for people in pain
j. belonging to a particular race or nation that has common customs and traditions

Discover the Story

1 When she was 7 years old, Milia Islam-Majeed and her family moved from Bangladesh to Fulton, Missouri, a small town in the middle of America. As a member of the only family of South Asians and Muslims living there, she learned at a young age what it felt like to be misunderstood by others who did not share the same religion or background as her.

2 However, it was in the busy and diverse city of Boston where Milia was most hurt by the religious intolerance of others. Her first day as a master's student at Harvard Divinity School was September 11, 2001: the day Islamic terrorists killed thousands of innocent people in New York.

3 Sadly, some Americans expressed their fear and anger toward the terrorism through violence toward American Muslims. As a Muslim woman wearing a headscarf, Milia became a target. Some Harvard students sent her e-mails full of hatred. In Boston's Harvard Square, people pulled at her headscarf, and when she was walking in a peace march, a man yelled out a window at her, "Go back to where you came from!" Sadly for her, despite having become an American citizen, she felt like "an outsider in [her] own home."

4 Some might have responded to this treatment by becoming angry themselves— but not Milia. She could see that the anger of others was "coming from an emotional place" rather than a place of clear thinking. She knew that when people learn about another person's faith, it is possible to become friends.

5 Milia put this belief into action, and today she is the Executive Director of Southern California's South Coast Interfaith Council, and the first Muslim to hold this position. Her job is to help people of different religions talk to, understand and be kind to one another, which is key to making life in Southern California fair and harmonious for all. Although it is one of the most diverse areas of the U.S. (California has the highest percentage of minorities of all

states), there were reportedly 489 "hate crimes" in Los Angeles County in 2011. These could be anything from graffiti on a place of worship to gang murder, since gangs are formed according to race and ethnicity. There are also cases of illegal discrimination, such as people refusing to hire or rent housing to someone of another faith or background.

6 In this environment, "interfaith cafes" can be very helpful. These are places where people can meet, discuss and compare religions over coffee and dessert. At the cafes, young people of different religions are invited to do charity work together and to get to know one another better as they build houses for the poor, clean up the beaches or help feed the homeless.

7 Additionally, Milia creates ways for different groups to share religious and cultural celebrations. Last year she organized an event attended by over 100 people, in which Japanese taiko drummers, Irish step dancers, Indian classical dancers, Balinese dancers and Latin folk dancers performed. She says these experiences are important because music and dance "transcend boundaries."

8 Milia often speaks about the challenges she faced as a Muslim in post-9/11 America, and her goals to help Americans understand each other's religions better—in Catholic churches, synagogues, Buddhist temples and mosques. One day at a synagogue, a Jewish woman told her that she hadn't thought listening to a Muslim person speak would change her opinion on Muslim-Jewish relations. But Milia's story inspired her so much that she said, "I want to put you in my pocket and take you home!"

9 Conversations like this one encourage Milia to keep working hard to help the coastal cities of Southern California become a "community of compassion." She encourages people to share their stories, for that is how to put "an image of yourself in the heart of another." As she says, "One story won't change the entire world, but it creates a trickle effect. Change happens one person at a time."

Notes **Fulton, Missouri**「ミズーリ州フルトン」アメリカ合衆国ミズーリ州の中央部北に位置するキャラウェイ群の郡庁所在地で、州都ジェファーソン市の一部でもある
Harvard Divinity School「ハーバード神学大学院」
Catholic churches「カトリック教会」　**synagogues**「シナゴーグ」ユダヤ教会堂
Buddhist temples「仏教寺院」　**mosques**「モスク」イスラム教の礼拝堂

Check Your Comprehension

 本文の内容について、質問に英語で答えましょう。
Answer each question in English.

1. What did Milia learn when she was young and living in Missouri in the United States?

   _____

2. Where was Milia most hurt by the religious intolerance of people?

   _____

3. What incident made Milia feel as if she were an "outsider in [her] own home"?

   _____

4. What is the job of the Executive Director of Southern California's South Coast Interfaith Council?

   _____

5. What do people do at "interfaith cafes"?

   _____

B 本文の内容について、質問の答えとして最も適切なものを選びましょう。
Choose the best answer for each question.

1. How did some Americans express their fear and anger toward terrorism?
    a. By being violent toward people of different religions
    b. By being violent toward people coming from foreign countries
    c. By being violent toward Asian Muslims
    d. By being violent toward American Muslims

2. What does "this belief" in the 5th paragraph mean?
    a. If people come from the same country, they can understand each other well.
    b. When people live close to each other, they can help each other.
    c. When people learn about another person's faith, they can become friends.
    d. If people meet often, it becomes easy to understand each other.

3. What is not an example of "hate crimes" in the 5th paragraph?
   a. Stealing money from your family
   b. Graffiti on church walls
   c. Gang murder
   d. Refusing to hire people of another faith

4. What did a Jewish woman tell Milia at a synagogue?
   a. Her opinion on Muslim-Jewish relations changed after listening to Milia's story.
   b. Her opinion on Muslim-Jewish relations didn't change after listening to Milia's story.
   c. She found her knowledge of Muslim-Jewish relations was better than Milia's.
   d. She found her knowledge of Muslim-Jewish relations was not enough.

5. How does Milia help the coastal cities of Southern California become a "community of compassion"?
   a. By encouraging people to go to religious meetings
   b. By encouraging people to share their stories
   c. By talking to each person about the challenges she faces
   d. By talking to people about different religions

C 本文の内容と一致していれば T と、一致していなければ F と答えましょう。
Mark each sentence true (T) or false (F).

1. Milia was angry when some people treated her as if she were not an American citizen. [ ]
2. Milia works hard to make life in Southern California fair and harmonious for all people. [ ]
3. Old and middle-aged people are invited to interfaith cafés. [ ]
4. Milia organizes cultural events because music and dance make it easy for people to go beyond their boundaries. [ ]
5. Milia believes that every little bit helps to make change happen. [ ]

Useful Expressions from the Story

空所に本文から適切な語を補い、英文を完成させましょう。
Fill in each blank with an appropriate word from the story.

1. She knew <u>what it felt _____ to be</u> treated in that way. [= how you would feel if you were]
2. One really begins to know oneself only _____ study. [= by means of]
3. He _____ <u>at the children</u> to be quiet. [= told the children very loudly]
4. Mike <u>put his plan into</u> _____. [= carried out his plan]
5. Matsuko was the first woman to _____ this position. [= have; occupy]

Your Thoughts on the Story

本文を読んで感じたことを、英語で書いてみましょう。必要に応じて、以下のフォーマットも活用しましょう。

Write down how you felt about the story after reading it. Use the format below if needed.

What I liked about the story is _____.

I was impressed by _____ because _____.

Also, I felt that _____.

After reading this story I thought _____.

本書には CD（別売）があります

Reading Trek!
英語で読む世界の 15 の物語

2019年1月20日 初版第1刷発行
2022年2月20日 初版第5刷発行

編著者　　栗　原　典　子
　　　　　Anthony Allan

発行者　　福　岡　正　人
発行所　　株式会社　金　星　堂
（〒101-0051）東京都千代田区神田神保町 3-21
　　　　　Tel.(03) 3263-3828（営業部）
　　　　　　　(03) 3263-3997（編集部）
　　　　　Fax (03) 3263-0716
　　　　　http://www.kinsei-do.co.jp

編集担当　松本明子　　　　　　　Printed in Japan
印刷所・製本所／株式会社カシヨ
本書の無断複製・複写は著作権法上での例外を除き禁じられています。本書を代行業者等の第三者に依頼してスキャンやデジタル化することは、たとえ個人や家庭内での利用であっても認められておりません。
落丁・乱丁本はお取り替えいたします。

ISBN978-4-7647-4081-5　C1082